ROSE
CHRONOLOGICAL
GUIDE TO THE BIBLE

Rose Chronological Guide to the Bible
©2019 Rose Publishing, LLC
Rose Publishing, LLC
P.O. Box 3473
Peabody, Massachusetts 01961-3473 USA
www.hendricksonrose.com

Contributing Authors: Jessica Curiel, Len Woods, Aaron Clay, Lisa Harlow Clay

Cover design by Sergio Urquiza; **page design** by Sergio Urquiza and Cristalle Kishi

Illustrations and Photographs: Stock images used under license from Shutterstock.com; Maps by Michael Schmeling www.aridocean.com; Jesus' Hours on the Cross by Hugh Claycombe.

Library of Congress Control Number:2019942803

Printed by Regent Publishing Services Ltd.
Shenzhen, China
May 2019, 1st printing

Contents

Introduction

Imagine rooting around in your grandparent's basement and finding a massive bundle of documents. There are old journals, business cards, assorted postcards from exotic places, some love letters, tattered newspaper clippings, baptismal and death certificates, marriage licenses, military awards, and lots of faded photos. You've just discovered a treasure trove of artifacts from your past! Think of all the stories that bundle represents—trips, jobs, weddings, illnesses, births, achievements, and funerals. And all together, those dusty old documents tell an even bigger story—the story of an entire family.

In a sense, that's what the Bible is. It's an ancient collection of sacred records that God supernaturally guided his people to write, preserve, and gather. When we peruse this holy anthology of writings, we find poetry, history, genealogies, verbal snapshots, and so much more. From Genesis to Revelation, we encounter hundreds of individual stories. And all together, these smaller stories comprise one big story—the story of God's people and God's love for the world.

How big a story are we talking? Try 750,000 words (give or take a few thousand depending on which Bible translation you've got). Maybe the mere thought of reading a story that epic intimidates you. Fear not, millions have done it, and you can too. And here's some help along the way. This chronological guide is designed to give you a quick, story-by-story overview of the Bible—the most read and most influential book of all time!

The Story of the Bible

Like all stories, the story of the Bible includes a few basic components. There are characters—the men, women, and families that the biblical story is about. There are also the characters of the spiritual realm—angels, demons, and the antagonist Satan. But the main character is God, his Son Jesus, and the Holy Spirit.

The setting of the story takes place mainly in the Middle East, Asia, and Europe, though we do get occasional peeks into heaven.

And don't forget, all stories include a conflict—a problem to be solved. What the characters do to overcome that problem is the plot of the story.

In the Bible, the conflict happens right at the beginning. God's beloved creatures and beautiful world are ruined by sin. Adam and Eve's rebellion brings the curse of sin and death into their perfect lives and pristine world. What will God do to rescue his rebellious creatures?

Shock of shocks, God handpicks an old, childless couple, Abraham and Sarah, and promises to make them into a great nation and bless the entire world through them! However, God's chosen family often fails to live as he commands. The Old Testament stories feature men and women who sometimes turn their hearts toward God, but other times turn their backs on him. Kingdoms and rulers rise and crumble. The curse of sin is not broken.

Then, after the last book of the Old Testament, nearly four centuries pass. The people of God find themselves at the mercy of foreign powers. They wonder: What about all those divine promises of a glorious future? Where is the Messiah that the prophets talked about?

Enter Jesus. This son born to Mary and Joseph of Nazareth is actually the Messiah promised in the Scriptures. Jesus is the unlikely hero of God's story. And what does Jesus do? He gathers followers. He claims to be divine. He tells people to put their faith in him. After living a sinless life, he willingly suffers an excruciating death on a Roman cross, offering his life as the payment for sin. He then defeats death, walking out of a borrowed grave! His followers take his message of love, forgiveness, and new life to the ends of the earth.

Most stories conclude with a resolution to the problem presented at the outset. Here's what's fascinating about God's story: The Bible's last book—Revelation—tells us that God's ultimate resolution is yet to come. The story isn't over. We get to play a part in God's holy plot to redeem and restore all things through Jesus Christ.

The Bible isn't simply "a bunch of documents from the past." It's that portion of God's story that the prophets and apostles recorded "as examples for us" (1 Cor. 10:11 NLT). Until Jesus returns, we get to add to the great, unfolding story. When Christ returns, he will conclude his two-part mission to vanquish evil and make all things new.

CHAPTER 1

The Beginning

From Creation to the Flood

All stories have a beginning. The story of the Bible starts not with the "once upon a time" of fairy tales, but with four other unforgettable words: "In the beginning God . . ." (Gen. 1:1). The biblical story begins with God. Before the existence of the world as we know it today, before millennia of human history, before even the formation of galaxies and planets, there was God.

Genesis, the first book of the Bible, is the account of how all good things in this world began, and how so much of it went terribly wrong.

Creation

Genesis 1–2

The first chapter of Genesis tells how God brought form to the formless and filled the emptiness with life. "Now the earth was formless and empty . . . and God said, 'Let there be light, and there was light'" (Gen. 1:2–3).

With the power of his word, God created light where there was none, put the galaxies in space, made birds to fill the air and fish to

GENESIS

Time/Place
Genesis covers from the creation of the world to the story of Joseph in Egypt around 1800 BC. The stories take place in Mesopotamia, Canaan, and Egypt.

The Book
Genesis is a book about beginnings. The word *genesis* comes from a Greek word meaning "to be born." Chapters 1–3 explain the origin of the world and humanity, followed by the origin of nations in chapters 4–11; and chapters 12–50 deal with the origin of Israel.

Key Verse
"In the beginning God created the heavens and the earth" (Gen. 1:1).

fill the seas, and like a potter at his wheel, he formed the first human being from the dust of the ground. What an extraordinary sight that must have been!

The creation story reveals who God is. He is the Creator who gives life to humanity and all living things. This world is his beautiful and "very good" creation (Gen. 1:31). In this story, we see God as designer, artist, architect, and life-giver; a good and loving God who takes delight in his creation.

There is a well-known speech by the apostle Paul in the New Testament in which he declares, "The God who made the world and everything in it is the Lord of heaven and earth and does not live in temples built by human hands. And he is not served by human hands, as if he needed anything. Rather, he himself gives everyone life and breath and everything else. From one man he made all the nations, that they should inhabit the whole earth" (Acts 17:24–26). Paul's words echo what the first chapter of the Bible teaches. God, the maker of all things, cannot be confined to a single place—not a mountain top, not a temple, not even a church building. He needs nothing, yet freely gives life to all.

The creation story also tells us something about ourselves. We are not here by accident. Our Creator purposefully designed us to reflect himself: "God created mankind in his own image, in the image of God he created them; male and female he created them" (Gen. 1:27). He made the first man, Adam, from the dust of the ground, and the first woman, Eve, from Adam's side. As image-bearers of God, their directive was an important one: to fill the earth and reign over God's creation.

Days of Creation Genesis 1:1–2:3

Days of Forming

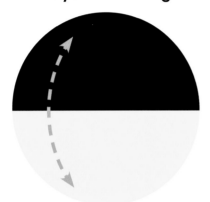

Day 1: God creates day and night by dividing light from the darkness.

Day 2: God creates the sky and waters by separating the waters.

Day 3: God creates the seas and dry land by gathering the waters together. God makes vegetation to grow on the land.

Days of Filling

Day 4: God creates the sun, moon, and stars to fill the day and the night.

Day 5: God creates birds to fill the skies and fish to fill the seas.

Day 6: God creates animals and humans to fill the land.

Day 7: God rests on the seventh day and blesses it and makes it holy.

A Fallen World

Genesis 3–5

The first two chapters of Genesis portray a picture of the world that is "very good" (Gen. 1:31). God put the first man and woman in the garden of Eden, a place where they cared for God's creation and God cared for them. Both Adam and Eve were naked and felt no shame (Gen. 2:25).

Consider the world as it is today. It's easy to see that many things are not the way they should be. If everything was once so good, how did it go so wrong? The next chapter in Genesis answers this question.

As image bearers of God, Adam and Eve had a choice: trust in the goodness of their creator or go their own way, rebelling against the kind of life God had given them. God issued them one restriction: "You must not eat from the tree of the knowledge of good and evil, for when you eat from it you will certainly die" (Gen. 2:17).

>>> ANGELS AND DEMONS

Though not mentioned in the Genesis creation narrative, other Bible passages reveal that God also created angels, holy messengers tasked to do his will (Ps. 148:2–5; Job 38:4–7).

We don't know exactly when, but sometime after creation and before Satan tempted Eve, a portion of the angels rebelled against their maker (2 Peter 2:4; Jude 6). The chief of these fallen angels is Satan, called the devil or the "prince of demons" (Matt. 12:22–32). In the end, God will completely and eternally defeat Satan and his demons (Matt. 25:41).

Deceived by a manipulative serpent, Eve chose the fruit of the one tree that was off-limits. (Revelation 12:9 and 20:2 point to the involvement of Satan—"that ancient serpent"—in this deception in the garden.) Adam also ate the fruit and things were never the same. Shame, followed by hiding from God, was their immediate response (Gen. 3:7–8). The man and woman had known only the goodness of God. In rebellion against their maker, they came to know evil as well.

They tried to hide from God, but it was no use. Sinful choices have consequences. Our decisions matter, just as they did for Adam and Eve. The first couple—and all humanity thereafter—was banished from the garden of Eden. Sinfulness, corruption, pain, and death entered the world. Life became very difficult—physical pain, hard work, broken relationships with each other and with God, and ultimately death. The world was no longer the way it should be.

The following stories in the book of Genesis give a clear—and at times disturbing—portrait of the effects of the sin. This is especially seen in the story of two of Adam and Eve's sons: Cain and Abel. Cain, jealous that Abel's sacrifice was accepted by God when his was not, plotted to kill his own brother. The sin of jealousy overtook Cain and he committed the first murder.

Life Spans from Adam to Abraham
Genesis 5:1–32; 11:10–26; 25:7

ADAM lived for 930 years.

SETH lived for 912 years.

ENOSH lived for 905 years.

KENAN lived for 910 years.

MAHALALEL lived for 895 years.

JARED lived for 962 years.

ENOCH lived for 365 years, then God took him.

METHUSELAH lived for 969 years.

LAMECH lived for 777 years.

NOAH lived for 950 years.

• **The Flood** (Noah at age 600)

SHEM lived for 600 years.

ARPHAXAD lived for 438 years.

SHELAH lived for 433 years.

EBER lived for 464 years.

PELEG lived for 239 years.

REU lived for 239 years.

SERUG lived for 230 years.

NAHOR lived for 148 years.

TERAH lived for 205 years.

ABRAHAM lived for 175 years.

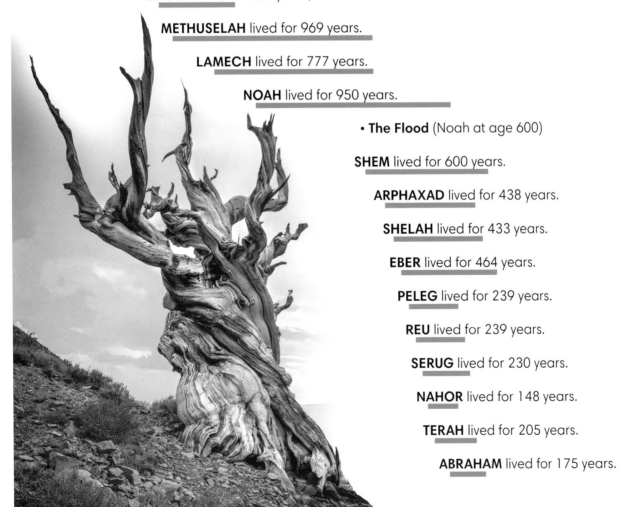

The lines in this chart indicate the length of the person's life in relation to the others.

Noah's Ark

Genesis 6–11

At this point in the biblical story, many years had passed since Adam and Eve, and the human race increased rapidly, but so did evil, corruption, and violence (Gen. 6:5, 12).

The creator who had given life in the first chapters of Genesis, here in chapter 6, concludes that the wickedness of humanity was so great that he would take away the all the life he had made on the face of the earth. The means of destruction would be a massive flood like the world had never seen before!

The flood story can be viewed as a kind of reverse creation story. It's the undoing of the created world that had become so corrupted.

Yet there was one man who had found favor with God. Noah, whose name means "comfort" or "relief," was a righteous and blameless person who walked with God (Gen. 6:8–9). God chose to save Noah and his family from his wrath against evil in the world. In a way, the life-destroying flood would bring about a new start for humanity, another beginning.

By faith, Noah did exactly as God instructed and built a large ark. Then, the flood waters came and covered the entire earth. For one year, Noah, his family, and many pairs of animals survived inside the ark. All other life on the land was destroyed. The breath of life we read about earlier in Genesis is snuffed out, save for a few on the ark. Finally, the waters receded and Noah and his family and all the animals exited the ark.

God made an everlasting covenant with Noah and all living creatures. He declared that never again would he destroy the earth in a flood. The rainbow in the sky would be the "sign of the covenant," a reminder that God will keep his promise (Gen. 9:12–17).

Though it was a new beginning, the fallen state of humanity and of the world continued. It wasn't long before Noah and his family were acting sinfully and reaping the consequences.

Chronology of the Flood
Genesis 7–8

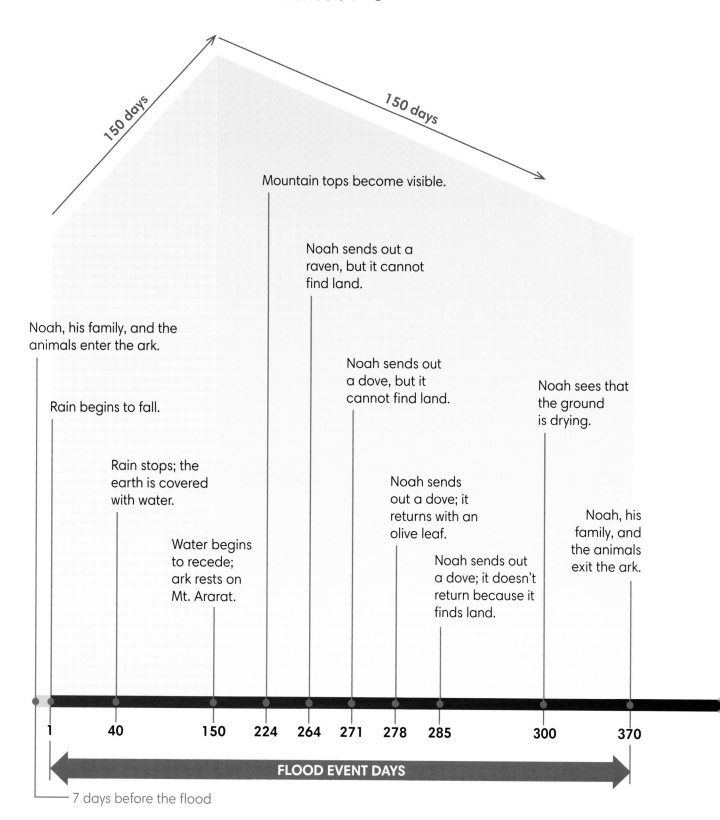

Noah, his family, and the animals enter the ark.

Rain begins to fall.

Rain stops; the earth is covered with water.

Water begins to recede; ark rests on Mt. Ararat.

Mountain tops become visible.

Noah sends out a raven, but it cannot find land.

Noah sends out a dove, but it cannot find land.

Noah sends out a dove; it returns with an olive leaf.

Noah sends out a dove; it doesn't return because it finds land.

Noah sees that the ground is drying.

Noah, his family, and the animals exit the ark.

150 days

150 days

| 1 | 40 | 150 | 224 | 264 | 271 | 278 | 285 | 300 | 370 |

FLOOD EVENT DAYS

7 days before the flood

Creation: In 6 days, God creates the world and human beings in his image.
Gen. 1–2

God rests on the 7th day.
Gen. 2:2

Adamic Covenant: God's promise to provide for his creation.
Gen. 1:26–30; 2:15–17

One day God will create a new heaven and a new earth. Rev. 21

Luke traces Jesus' genealogy all the way back to the first human, Adam. Luke 3:38

The book of Hebrews speaks of a true Sabbath-rest of peace for those who trust in Jesus. Heb. 4:1–11

At God's instruction, Noah builds an ark.
Gen. 6

Noah, his family, and pairs of every kind of animal enter the ark.
Gen. 7:1–5

The Flood: God sends a flood to cover the earth.
Gen. 7:6–24

The flood waters recede. Noah, his family, and the animals exit the ark.
Gen. 8:1–19

The book of Hebrews lists Noah as an example of faith for building the ark by trusting what God had told him. Heb. 11:7

As Noah and his family were saved from death in the flood, so we are saved by Jesus and his resurrection from the dead. 1 Peter 3:20–22

The Fall: Adam and Eve break God's command by eating from the Tree of the Knowledge of Good and Evil. Gen. 3:1–7

God banishes Adam and Eve from the garden of Eden. Gen. 3:8–34

Cain kills his brother Abel: the first murder. Gen. 4

Population increases and so does sinfulness. Gen. 5–6

In the book of Revelation, the serpent who deceived Eve is identified as Satan. Rev. 12:9; 20:2

Paul explains that death and sin entered the world through one man. But death is not the final word: "As in Adam all die, so in Christ all will be made alive." Rom. 5:12; 1 Cor. 15:22

Genesis 3:15 points to the coming of Jesus who will defeat Satan: "I will put enmity between you [the serpent] and the woman, and between your offspring and hers; he will crush your head, and you will strike his heel." See also Heb. 2:14; 1 John 3:8

Noahic Covenant: Never again will God destroy the earth in a flood; rainbow is the sign of the covenant. Gen. 8:20–9:17

Noah plants a vineyard and gets drunk. Gen. 9:18–29

Noah's descendants populate the earth. Gen. 10

At the Tower of Babel, God confuses language and scatters the people. Gen. 11

In his vision of God's heavenly throne room, John sees a magnificent rainbow. Rev. 4:3

Noah and his son Shem are listed in the genealogy of Jesus. Luke 3:36

TIME LINE KEY

 Prophecy Fulfilled by Jesus

 Person in the Genealogy of Jesus

 New Testament Connection

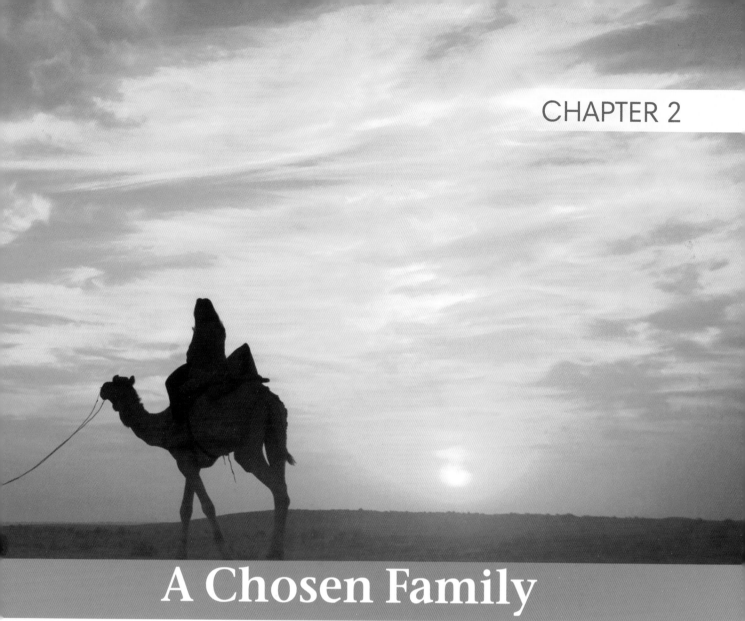

CHAPTER 2

A Chosen Family

From Abraham to Joseph
2100–1800 BC

Abraham and Sarah

Joseph in Egypt

The Story of Job

Covenants in the Bible

Even with a new beginning after the flood waters were gone, sin and corruption remained in the world. Much of humanity continued living against the will of God. Yet, as the stories in Genesis reveal, God was undeterred from bringing about his plan to redeem humanity and all creation. Starting in Genesis 12, we see God forging a path of redemption through one special—though far from perfect—family. The story of this family begins with a childless couple named Abraham and Sarah.

Abraham and Sarah

Genesis 12–24

Abraham and his wife Sarah (also called Abram and Sarai) were originally from the ancient city of Ur in Mesopotamia. Ur, as we know from archaeology, was a thriving center of commerce located along the Euphrates River in modern-day Iraq. It was also a city teeming with the worship of false gods. Abraham's family was semi-nomadic, moving to wherever they could find food and pasturelands for their flocks. They traveled from Ur to Harran in upper Mesopotamia, another major city of commerce.

God called Abraham to migrate from Harran to the land of Canaan. God assured Abraham with a covenant—like a promise or pledge—that God would bless him and his family. Throughout Abraham's story in Genesis, God reaffirms this covenant with Abraham on seven different occasions. The covenant included these promises: Abraham and Sarah would have a son (Gen. 18:1–15); all nations would be blessed through Abraham's descendants (Gen. 12:1–3); the land that

God would show Abraham would belong to his descendants (Gen. 12:7; 22:15–18); and Abraham's descendants would be as numerous as the stars in the sky and the sand on the seashore (Gen. 13:14–17; 15:1–21; 17:1–21; 22:17).

By faith, Abraham and his family left a thriving pagan city and followed God into a new and strange land. Genesis tells us that Abraham's faith in God's promise was "credited to him as righteousness" (Gen. 15:6). The book of Hebrews in the New Testament explains it this way: "By faith

The Caravan of Abram
by James Tissot, c. 1903

Abraham, when called to go to a place he would later receive as his inheritance, obeyed and went, even though he did not know where he was going. By faith he made his home in the promised land like a stranger in a foreign country. . . . For he was looking forward to the city with foundations, whose architect and builder is God" (Heb. 11:8–10).

But there was a problem—at least from a human point of view. Abraham and Sarah were old and childless. How could they have a multitude of descendants, let alone even one descendant? God was promising them the impossible.

In the ancient world, infertility was considered cause for a husband to divorce his wife or to have heirs through concubines or slaves. Rather than continue to wait for God's promise to be fulfilled, Abraham, at Sarah's urging, had a son through Sarah's slave, Hagar. Despite their attempt to shortcut God's promises, God kept his covenant, and Sarah, well-advanced in age, bore a son, Isaac. God was faithful to the covenant, but it was according to his timetable, not theirs. In fact, Isaac was born a full twenty-five years after God had first made the covenant with Abraham (Gen. 12:4; 21:5).

Abraham's faith in God must have increased after Isaac's birth, because when God told Abraham to do the unthinkable—to sacrifice his only son Isaac—Abraham was willing. Before Abraham could go through with it, God stopped him and provided a ram as the sacrifice instead. In this divine test, Abraham demonstrated great faith, believing that "God could even raise the dead" (Heb. 11:19).

As we learn from the rest of the Bible, God's plan was even bigger than what Abraham and Sarah may have understood. Not only would their descendants be numerous, but the Messiah, Jesus the Savior, would be born through Abraham's lineage. Remember that Genesis is a book of beginnings; it tells not only the beginning of the nation of Israel through a son promised to Abraham and Sarah, but it also explains the beginning of a history which would ultimately lead to Christ Jesus, the Son of God.

COVENANTS

The Old Testament word for covenant is *berit*, which likely comes from a Hebrew verb meaning "to bind." A covenant is a binding relationship, like a very serious promise, contract, oath, or treaty. But it's more than just a business agreement; it involves a personal relationship that requires trust. For example, marriage is referred to as covenant in Malachi 2:14.

Sometimes covenants were accompanied by a sign, such as a rainbow in God's covenant with Noah (Gen. 9:13) or the cup of the new covenant in Jesus' blood (Luke 22:20).

Hebrews 10:1 explains that Old Testament covenants were but "shadows of the good things that are coming." Jesus fulfilled these covenants and instituted a new, eternal covenant with all who follow him (Heb. 9:15).

Jacob's Family

Genesis 25–36

After Abraham's and Sarah's deaths, the biblical narrative turns to Isaac's twin sons, Jacob and Esau, but particularly Jacob. At birth, Jacob was given his name, translated as "he grasps at the heel," an ancient Hebrew expression that meant "he deceives" (Gen. 25:26). Later in Jacob's life, God changed his name to Israel which means "struggles with God" (Gen. 32:28). Both names suggest a man (and also a family) in a tug-of-war with God and each other.

The stories in this section of Genesis detail how God's chosen family struggled. They struggled with God—Jacob did so, literally in Genesis 32. They struggled with each other—deceiving, fearing, and betraying. Some were victims, others were victimizers, and some were both. Most times they focused on their own survival, status, and power. For example, Jacob and his mother Rebekah tricked an aged and blind Isaac into giving Jacob the blessing that belonged to Esau (Gen. 27:1–45). Jacob fled when Esau vowed revenge. It would be twenty years before the brothers would meet again. Jacob was fooled by Laban, who tricked him into marrying Leah when Jacob had wanted to marry Rachel. The deceiver had become the deceived. In the end, Jacob married both sisters (Gen. 29:15–30). (Having multiple wives was a common practice in the ancient world.) Leah and Rachel competed for their husband's affection by having as many children for him as possible—twelve sons and one daughter in total. They even gave

their slave women to their husband to have children through them, much like Sarah had done with Hagar two generations earlier (Gen. 29:31–30:24).

There were, however, times when this family turned toward God, and God turned toward them. Jacob received an amazing glimpse into the heavenly realm, a dream of a stairway to heaven. The Lord reassured Jacob that the promises made to his grandfather Abraham would be fulfilled. An awestruck Jacob declared, "How awesome is this place! . . . The LORD will be my God" (Gen. 28:10–22). After twenty years of estrangement from his brother Esau, Jacob returned to Canaan and encountered Esau. Fearing for his life, Jacob humbled himself and prayed to God for protection. Much to Jacob's surprise, Esau did not take revenge, but instead embraced and forgave Jacob (Gen. 32:1–33:4). The Lord renewed his covenantal promises of blessing with this family despite their repeated failings (Gen. 26:3–5; 28:13–15). God chose to work his will through their broken lives, rescuing them from certain doom when their lies and foolishness got them in trouble.

Joseph in Egypt

Genesis 37–50

Against the backdrop of this very flawed family, the story of Joseph stands out. The book of Genesis devotes thirteen chapters (that's about one fourth of the book) to the story of Joseph. His story provides us with an example of a young man from an unstable family who chose to rely on God when so much of his future seemed hopeless.

Isaac blessing Jacob
by Govert Flinck, 1638

Joseph's older brothers resented him. As the biological son of Rachel, the wife Jacob loved most, Joseph was favored by his father. Also, God gave Joseph special dreams, which Joseph unwisely relayed to his brothers. His brothers understood Joseph's dreams to mean that one day they would all bow down to him—their little brother! Joseph's brothers were determined to make sure that would never happen. They sold him to slave traders and told their father that Joseph had been killed by a wild animal.

As a slave in Egypt, Joseph had no connections, no money, no status, and no protection from harm. But he did have one person on his side: "The LORD was with Joseph" (Gen. 39:2, 3, 21, 23). That made all the difference. Joseph didn't just survive in this foreign land, he thrived. He was put in charge of the whole household of Potiphar, one of Pharaoh's officers.

But then Joseph suffered another injustice. He was thrown into prison after Potiphar's wife falsely accused him. He had done no wrong but once again found himself in chains. Yet the Lord was still with him. God gave Joseph the ability to correctly interpret dreams—a blessing for which he gave God all the credit (Gen. 41:16). Joseph interpreted Pharaoh's dream about seven years of good harvest followed by seven years of famine. Pharaoh was so impressed that he released Joseph from prison and put him in charge of storing food for the people to survive the coming famine. Joseph became a top official in Egypt. The Lord was indeed with Joseph.

When his brothers traveled to Egypt to buy food during the famine, Joseph was faced with a choice: forgiveness or revenge. Unlike some others in his family tree had done before, Joseph chose forgiveness. He tested his brothers' sincerity and character with some deceit of his own, hiding his true identity. But in the end, he stopped the deception, revealed who he really was, and forgave his brothers entirely. Joseph understood that God had a bigger plan that would succeed in spite of human sinfulness. He declared to his brothers, "You intended to harm me, but God intended it for good to accomplish what is now being done, the saving of many lives" (Gen. 50:20).

This part of the biblical story—and the book of Genesis—ends with God's chosen family living in Egypt. Jacob and his family had migrated to Egypt to escape the famine. Though they grew in number, as God's covenant said they would, they were far from the land God had promised. We read in the last chapter of Genesis that, though Joseph had made a new home for himself in Egypt, he wanted to be buried in the promised land (Gen. 50:25). This demonstrated Joseph's trust that God would be faithful to fulfill the promises he made so many years earlier to Abraham.

Journeys of the Patriarchs

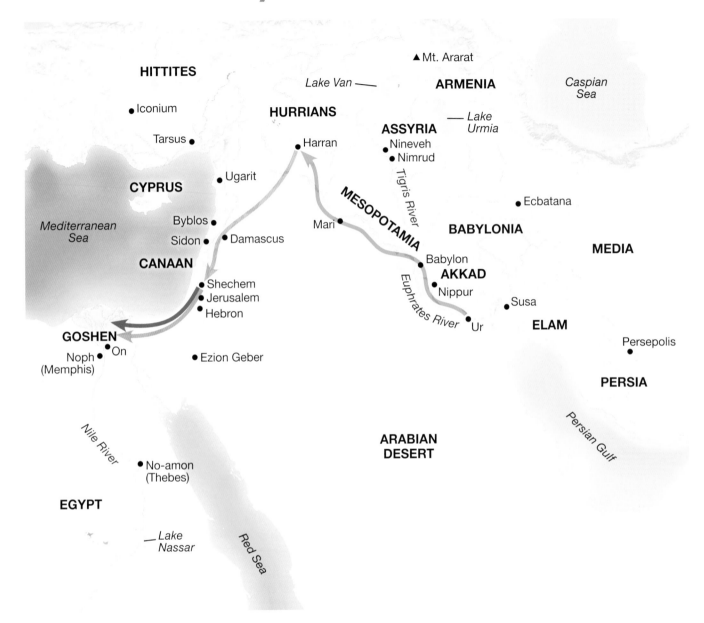

1. Terah moves his family (Abraham, Sarah, Lot) from Ur to Harran. Gen. 11:31–32

2. Obeying God's calling, Abraham, Sarah, and Lot move from Harran to Canaan. Gen. 12:1–9

3. Abraham and Sarah go to Egypt to escape a famine, then return to Canaan. Gen. 12:10–20

4. Joseph, Jacob's eleventh son, is taken by slave traders to Egypt. About 21 years later, the rest of Jacob's family migrates to Egypt. Gen. 37:25–28; 47:27

Genealogy of Abraham's Family

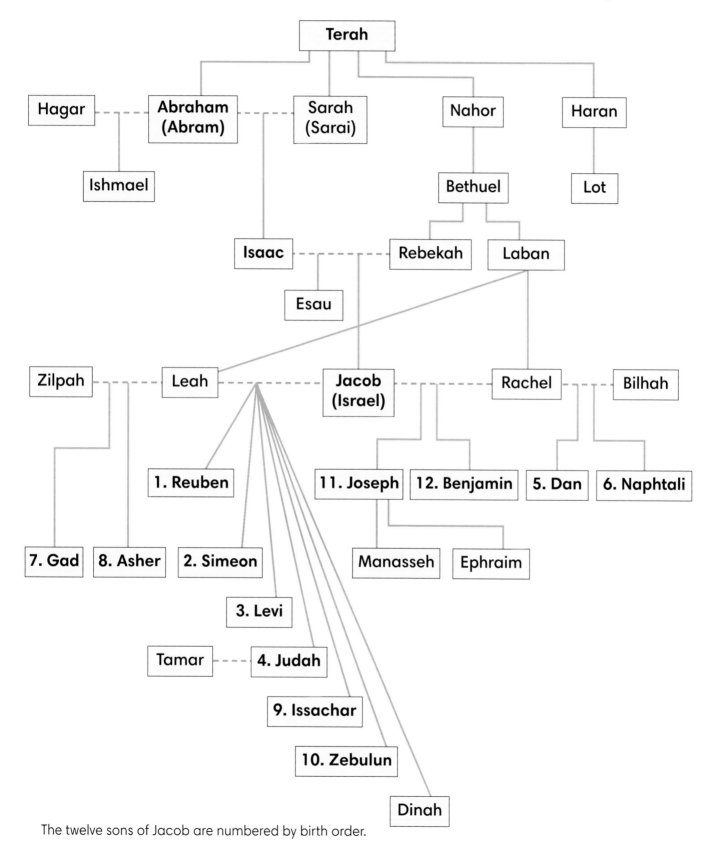

The twelve sons of Jacob are numbered by birth order.

The Story of Job

The book of Job tells the story of an upright man whose life is overthrown. Job is a good man with a good life, and yet God permits Satan to take it all away. Job loses everything: his riches, his children, and his health—everything but his loyalty to God.

Clues from the book suggest that Job lived sometime during the era of the patriarchs (Abraham, Isaac, Jacob) possibly in Edom, east of the Dead Sea. But no matter when or where Job lived, his story invites all readers to ponder the universal human experience of suffering.

In the story, we see Job's friends trying to empathize with him, but their speeches always end in accusations. Various passages in the Old Testament correctly teach that if you sin, then you will suffer (see for example, Deut. 30:16–18; Prov. 11:21). Job's friends, however, turn this teaching on its head. They argue that if you are suffering, then you must have sinned. Job's ordeal shows how their assumption is wrong.

Job's story also illustrates the limits of human understanding. In chapter one, Job is unaware of the conversations happening in the celestial court between God and Satan that will upend his life. When God finally speaks to Job near the end of the book, God doesn't answer Job's questions about why he is suffering. We, like Job, often don't fully know what God is doing behind the scenes of our lives, or why.

In the end, Job comes to trust that God still loves him and cares for him despite his suffering. Trusting in God's love turns out to be a better comfort than getting all the answers we think we need.

The book closes with God restoring Job's health and riches and blessing him with more children. This serves as a reminder that suffering is temporary (though it might seem endless at the time) and that the God who permitted calamity can and will bring healing and blessing. As James says in the New Testament, "You have heard of Job's perseverance and have seen what the Lord finally brought about. The Lord is full of compassion and mercy" (James 5:11).

Job

Time/Place
Job's story may have occurred during the era of Abraham, Isaac, and Jacob in an unknown location simply called "the land of Uz" (Job 1:1), possibly Edom.

The Book
Job is written in a style of ancient Hebrew known as wisdom literature. Rather than dealing directly with Israel's history, wisdom literature—like Job, Psalms, Proverbs—reflects on universal themes and overarching questions that are relevant for all people in all places. The beginning and end of Job are written in prose (Job 1:1–2:13; 42:7–17), with everything in between written in poetry.

Key Verse
"The Lord gave and the Lord has taken away; may the name of the Lord be praised" (Job 1:21).

Job and His Friends
by Ilya Repin, 1869

Covenants in the Bible

Adamic Covenant

Gen. 1:26–30; 2:15–17

Who: God, Adam and Eve, all creation

When: At creation

What: Provision for all God's creation

Noahic Covenant

Gen. 8:20–9:17

Who: God, Noah, every living creature

When: After the flood

What: Never again destroy the world in a flood

Abrahamic Covenant

Gen. 12:1–7

Who: God, Abraham

When: Abraham at age 75; 2091 BC

What: Descendants and the promised land

Mosaic Covenant

Ex. 19:3–8

Who: God, Moses, Israel

When: After the exodus; 1446 BC (or 1290 BC)

What: Blessings if Israel obeys God's law

Davidic Covenant

2 Sam. 7:4–17

Who: God, King David

When: David's reign; 1000 BC

What: Establish David's throne forever

New Covenant

Jer. 31:31–34; Matt. 26:28; Heb. 8:6

Who: God, Jesus, all who trust in Jesus

When: Jesus' death and resurrection; AD 30

What: New relationship, eternal life, superior covenant

The story of Job.
Job 1–42

Abram's father moves his family from Ur to Harran.
Gen. 11

Abrahamic Covenant: God calls Abram to move to Canaan. Abram obeys.
Gen. 12:1–9

2091 BC

In Egypt, Abram tells Pharaoh that Sarai is his sister. God intervenes and rescues Sarai.
Gen. 12:10–20

Abram rescues his nephew Lot from captivity.
Gen. 13–14

2100 BC

James mentions Job's story as an example of perseverance and of God's compassion in restoring Job.
James 5:11

Through Abraham's descendants all nations would be blessed. Through Jesus Christ, a descendant of Abraham, all nations are blessed. Gen. 12:3; Matt. 28:18–20; Acts 28:28

Abraham tells Abimelek that Sarah is his sister. God intervenes and rescues Sarah.
Gen. 20

Isaac is miraculously born to Abraham and Sarah.
Gen. 21

2066 BC

Abraham sends Hagar and Ishmael away, but God provides for them.
Gen. 21

God tests Abraham by telling him to sacrifice Isaac. God provides a ram as the sacrifice instead.
Gen. 22

Sarah dies at age 127.
Gen. 23

2050 BC

Isaac is listed in Jesus' genealogy. Matt. 1:2; Luke 3:34

Abraham's attempted sacrifice of Isaac took place on Mount Moriah near Jerusalem. God substituted a ram in place of Isaac. Jesus was crucified on the outskirts of Jerusalem as the sacrifice who substituted himself for us. Gen. 22:2; 2 Chron. 3:1; John 19:17–18

Abram gives a tithe (a tenth) to the king and priest Melchizedek. Gen. 14–15

Sarai gives her slave Hagar to Abram. Hagar bears a son Ishmael. Gen. 16

God renames Abram and Sarai: Abraham ("father of many") and Sarah ("princess"). Gen. 17

Three celestial visitors declare that Sarah will bear a son within one year. Gen. 18

God destroys Sodom and Gomorrah but spares Lot. Gen. 19

The book of Hebrews explains how Jesus is the High Priest for eternity in the order of Melchizedek. Heb. 5–7

Though they often lacked faith, both Abraham and Sarah are listed in the book of Hebrews as examples of faith for the times when they did trust God to fulfill his promises. Heb. 11:8, 11

Abraham's servant finds a wife for Isaac: Rebekah. Gen. 24

Rebekah bears twin sons: Esau and Jacob. Gen. 25:19–26

2005 BC

Abraham dies at age 175. Gen. 25:1–18

1991 BC

Esau sells his birthright to Jacob for a bowl of stew. Gen. 25:27–34

Isaac lies about his wife, saying she is his sister. Gen. 26

2000 BC

Jacob is listed in Jesus' genealogy. Matt. 1:2; Luke 3:34

TIME LINE KEY

 Prophecy Fulfilled by Jesus

 Person in the Genealogy of Jesus

 New Testament Connection

Dates are approximate.

Rebekah and Jacob trick Isaac into giving Jacob the blessing of the firstborn.
Gen. 27

Esau vows revenge. Jacob flees to Harran. He has a dream of a stairway to heaven.
Gen. 28

Jacob marries Leah and Rachel.
Gen. 29

Jealous for their husband's affection, Leah and Rachel compete by having sons.
Gen. 30–31

On his way back to Canaan, Jacob wrestles with the angel of the Lord and is renamed Israel ("struggles with God").
Gen. 32

Jesus alluded to Jacob's stairway when he declared himself to be the pathway between heaven and earth. John 1:51

Jesus was a descendant of Judah, the fourth son of Jacob born to Leah. Matt. 1:2; Luke 3:33

Judah sleeps with his widowed daughter-in-law Tamar.
Gen. 38

Joseph is thrown into prison after Potiphar's wife falsely accuses him.
Gen. 39

Joseph interprets dreams in prison.
Gen. 40

Joseph is made a top official when he interprets Pharaoh's dream.
Gen. 41

Joseph's brothers travel to Egypt to buy grain during a famine.
Gen. 42–43

Tamar is one of five women listed in Matthew's account of the genealogy of Jesus. Matt. 1:3

After 20 years of estrangement, Jacob and Esau reconcile.
Gen. 33

Dinah is assaulted by a local city ruler's son. Her brothers take revenge on the city.
Gen. 34

Rachel dies while giving birth to Benjamin.
Gen. 35

Isaac dies at age 180.
Gen. 35

Joseph's jealous brothers sell him to slave traders who take him to Egypt.
Gen. 37

1900 BC

Stephen, the first Christian martyr, retold the story of Joseph as he built the case that Jesus is truly the Messiah. Acts 7:9–16

Joseph tests his brothers, reveals his identity, and forgives them.
Gen. 44–45

Jacob's family settles in Egypt.
Gen. 46

1876 BC

Joseph supplies food for the masses during a 7-year famine.
Gen. 47

Jacob blesses his sons before his death.
Gen. 48–49

Joseph dies in Egypt at age 110.
Gen. 50

1805 BC

1800 BC

God worked through Joseph's hardships to save many lives. In Jesus, God offers salvation to all people through Jesus' death on the cross "for the sins of the whole world." Gen. 50:20; 1 John 2:2

The book of Hebrews lists Jacob as an example of faith for blessing his descendants.
Heb. 11:20–21

Jacob's blessing to Judah was that "the scepter will not depart from Judah," indicating an everlasting kingship.
Gen. 49:10; Luke 1:33

CHAPTER 3

A Redeemed People

From Egypt to the Wilderness
1800–1400 BC

The exodus is the story of how God redeemed his people from slavery in Egypt and brought them to the land promised to Abraham, Isaac, and Jacob. This journey was not a straight or easy path. It was winding and dangerous, both physically and spiritually. For forty years they lived as nomads in the desert. God had told them the big plan: he would be their God who frees them from captivity and provides for their needs. But God didn't tell them the details. He only required that at each stage of the journey they trust him, following his guidance wherever he led them.

Moses and the Exodus

Exodus 1–18

The book of Exodus opens with the descendants of Jacob (called Hebrews or Israelites) growing numerous in the land of Egypt for many years. God had blessed them, but the Egyptian rulers saw their success as a threat and became suspicious.

> Then a new king, to whom Joseph meant nothing, came to power in Egypt. "Look," he said to his people, "the Israelites have become far too numerous for us. Come, we must deal shrewdly with them or they will become even more numerous and, if war breaks out, will join our enemies, fight against us and leave the country. So they put slave masters over them to oppress them with forced labor." (Ex. 1:8–11)

Their masters "worked them ruthlessly" (Ex. 1:13). Even worse, to prevent further population growth, Pharaoh ordered every Hebrew newborn boy to be thrown into the Nile River! It was during this time that a Hebrew baby named Moses was born. Moses was miraculously saved from death in the Nile and raised by Pharaoh's daughter. He grew up as a member of Pharaoh's household, but God had chosen Moses for something much greater than the royal Egyptian court.

As an adult, Moses' life took an unexpected turn when he was forced to flee Egypt as a fugitive. He settled in the distant land of Midian as a shepherd, ready to live the rest of his life in obscurity. But one day, while Moses was tending flocks, God called to him from a burning bush: "Moses! Moses!" (Ex. 3:4). Moses' divine directive was to go back to Egypt and confront Pharaoh to let God's people leave Egypt. At first, Moses balked at the enormity of the task in comparison to his own weakness: "Who am I that I should go to Pharaoh and bring the Israelites out of Egypt?" (Ex. 3:11). But as the apostle Paul teaches in the New Testament, God's grace is sufficient and his power is made complete in human weakness: "For when I am weak, then I am strong" (2 Cor. 12:9–10). Moses became a great leader because his God was great.

Moses, along with his brother Aaron, went back to Egypt and confronted Pharaoh, the ruler of the most powerful kingdom the ancient world had known. The Egyptians considered Pharaoh to be the "son of Ra" and a god of Egypt who was responsible for maintaining cosmic order. Moses' initial fear and hesitancy to challenge Pharaoh make sense. Moses was confronting an Egyptian deity! On the surface, Moses and Aaron were facing off against Pharaoh and his magicians; yet it was really the God of Moses facing the false gods of the Egyptians.

God sent nine terrible plagues upon Egypt, but after each one, Pharaoh refused to let the Israelites leave. The Lord hardened Pharaoh's heart to prove to Pharaoh, Egypt, and the Israelites that he alone is the one true God (Ex. 4:21; 7:3; 10:20, 27; 14:4). "When the Israelites saw the mighty hand of the LORD displayed against the Egyptians, the people feared the LORD and put their trust in him" (Ex. 14:31).

The tenth and final plague was the worst: the death of firstborn sons. Pharaoh had killed the newborn sons of Israel; now God was about to put to death the sons of Egypt. Only households with the blood of a perfect lamb spread across their doorframes would be untouched by this plague. The Lord's

hand passed over those houses, sparing them from death.

When Pharaoh's own son died in the tenth plague, he relented and let God's people leave. The descendants of Abraham, Isaac, and Jacob left Egypt, and they took with them the bones of Joseph to bury in the promised land—a pledge made four hundred years earlier (Gen. 50:25; Ex. 13:19).

From Egypt to Mount Sinai, God continued to demonstrate his goodness and might by providing for and protecting his people. He guided their route with a pillar of cloud by day and pillar of fire by night (Ex. 13:21–22). When the Egyptian army pursued them, God parted the sea for the Israelites to pass through on dry ground and destroyed Pharaoh's army with walls of water crashing in on them (Ex. 14:1–31). He provided manna and quail for food in desert, just enough for each day (Ex. 16:13–18). After three months of travelling in the wilderness, God led the Israelites to the base of Mount Sinai.

Death of the Pharaoh's Firstborn Son by Lawrence Alma-Tadema, 1872

The Ten Plagues

Exodus 12:12 states that God's judgment through the tenth plague came upon "all the gods of Egypt" (see also Num. 33:4). Archaeologists are not certain about which particular deities were being worshiped in Egypt during the time of the exodus. Much of the information about Egyptian gods actually comes from a different time period and location in Egyptian history. Despite this uncertainty, it's still beneficial to consider possible connections between the plagues and the Egyptian deities since through the plagues, God was revealing his power over all things.

Plague	Description	Egyptian gods
Water into Blood Ex. 7:14–25	The Nile River turned into blood. This was the primary source of water in the land and the heart of Egyptian life.	*Hapi*: god of the annual flooding of the Nile. *Khnum*: god of the source of the Nile.
Frogs Ex. 8:1–15	Frogs invaded everything, eventually dying and unleashing foul smells throughout the land.	*Heqet*: goddess of fertility and childbirth, represented as a frog.
Gnats/Lice Ex. 8:16–19	Dust turned into small insects, possibly gnats or lice. The Egyptian priests could not duplicate this plague like the others.	*Geb*: god of the earth; gnats came from the "dust of the earth."
Flies/ Mosquitoes Ex. 8:20–32	The precise identity of these flying insects is unclear. Psalm 78:45 suggests that the insects fed on the Egyptians.	*Khepri*: god of the rising son, represented with the head of a fly or scarab beetle.
Death of Livestock Ex. 9:1–7	A plague was sent on the Egyptian livestock in the fields. The Israelites' livestock was unharmed.	*Hathor*: mother and sky goddess, represented by a cow. *Apis*: portrayed as a sacred bull sacrificed and then reborn.
Boils Ex. 9:8–12	Boils appeared on both the Egyptians and their animals. Egyptian priests/healers could do nothing to help.	*Imhotep*: god of healing/medicine. *Sekhmet*: goddess of healing.
Hail Ex. 9:13–35	A hailstorm struck Egyptians lands. Some of Pharaoh's officials sided with Moses after this plague.	*Seth*: god of storms and disorder. *Nut*: goddess of the sky.
Locusts Ex. 10:1–20	Locusts ate every plant not destroyed in the hailstorm. Egyptian officials pleaded with Pharaoh to listen to Moses.	*Serapia*: god with the head of a locust who protected against locusts.
Darkness Ex. 10:21–29	Intense darkness descended upon the land for three days; so dark that it was described as if it could be touched.	*Ra, Amon-ra, Atum, Horus*: gods associated with the sun.
Death of Firstborn Ex. 11:1–12:30	God struck dead all firstborn males including Pharaoh's son. But those with lamb's blood on their doorframes were spared (Passover).	This plague was an attack on the linage and deity of Pharaoh himself.

The Date of the Exodus

Dating of the exodus event is very difficult and highly debated. There are two main options: a high date (1446 BC) and a low date (1290 BC).

Evidence for the High Date (1446 BC)

♦ First Kings 6:1 states that the exodus happened 480 years before Solomon's fourth year (966 BC). Working backward, this dates the exodus at 1446 BC.

♦ In Judges 11:26, Jephthah (around 1100 BC) claimed that Israel had been in Canaan for 300 years. Adding 40 years for the wilderness journey, this places the exodus around 1440 BC.

♦ The Amarna Letters/Tablets (around 1400 BC) are correspondence written between Egyptian officials and representatives in Canaan. These letters speak of a period of chaos in Canaan, which could be Joshua's conquest 40 years after the exodus. The letters also make mention of a group referred to in Akkadian as the *hapiru*—social outcasts/ nomads, slaves, or migrant workers— possibly the Israelites at that time.

♦ The Merneptah Stele (around 1220 BC) is an inscription recounting an Egyptian ruler's victories. The stele makes mention of "Israel" as an established group in Canaan. The low date of 1290 BC does not provide enough time for Israel to be well established by the date of this stele.

♦ The Dream Stele (1401 BC) indicates that Thutmose IV was not the firstborn legal heir to the throne, hinting at the idea that the firstborn son of Amenhotep II (1453–1426 BC) had died.

Evidence for the Low Date (1290 BC)

♦ No references to "Israel" as a people have been discovered outside the Bible prior to the Merneptah Stele.

♦ The cities that the Bible says the Hebrews built while in Egypt (Pithom and Rameses; Ex. 1:11) were completed by Ramses II (1304–1237 BC).

♦ Biblical dating can be understood as symbolic, so the 480 years mentioned in 1 Kings 6:1 is a period of 12 generations (40 years per generation). Biblical dates may also be exaggerated or generalized, such as Jephthah's claim of 300 years (Judg. 11:26).

♦ The time frames for the various judges mentioned in the book of Judges may have overlapped. This would account for a shorter period of time for Joshua's conquest, settlement, and the era of judges, making a low date possible.

As new archaeological discoveries are made, our understanding of this time period continues to grow. While there is not enough evidence to say for certain that the high date of the exodus is correct, both tradition and current research support this position more favorably than the low date. (The time line presented in this book follows the traditional high date.)

Merneptah Stele
MartinEvans/Shutterstock.com

The Route of the Exodus

The Bible provides a fairly detailed list of the Israelites' movements from Egypt to Sinai (Ex. 12:37–19:2; Num. 33:1–15). However, many of the locations are uninhabited sites and identifying them in both the ancient and modern context can be difficult, if not impossible. Scholars have done their best to piece together the information found in the Bible along with the archaeological sites and have proposed three main options:

Southern Route: The Israelites left Goshen and headed south through the Sinai Peninsula. Traditionally, Mount Sinai is located near the southern tip of the peninsula at Jebel Musa, though some suggest it's a little farther north near the Desert of Sin at Jebel Serbal.

Central Route: The Israelites took a more central route across the middle of the Sinai Peninsula. In this view, Mount Sinai is located in Arabia/Midian at Jabal al-Lawz east of the Sinai Peninsula or at Jebel Sin Bisher in Sinai. Potential problems with this view include the harshness of the route (lack of water) and the amount of time it would take to reach the crossing point into Arabia.

Northern Route: The Israelites headed north, with Mount Sinai in the northwestern area of the Sinai Peninsula at Jebel-Helal. However, this view does not take into account that Scripture says God led Israel away from the Philistines located along the Mediterranean coast (Ex. 13:17–18). It is also inconsistent with the eleven-day journey mentioned in Deuteronomy 1:2.

Where Was the "Red Sea"?

Traditionally, the Israelites are said to have crossed the "Red Sea" as they fled from Egypt (Ex. 13:18). This is based on the Greek translation of the Hebrew phrase *yam suph*. But is this what the Hebrew really says? The Hebrew word *yam* can be used for any large body of water like a sea or even a lake. *Suph* in Hebrew is actually the word for "reed," not "red." This same term is used to describe where Moses' basket was placed in the Nile (Ex. 2:3, 5). Based on the Old Testament's use of this word, a more accurate translation for *yam suph* is likely "reed sea" or "sea of reeds."

The more pressing question is where was this sea located? The traditional southern route puts the sea at the tip of the Red Sea/Gulf of Suez. Also, the detailed list of places the Israelites camped says that after crossing the *yam suph* they stayed at Marah, then Elim, and then they camped by the *yam suph* again (Num. 33:8–10). If they camped next to the same body of water again, it would have to be a very large body of water, not a small lake.

Other suggested locations for *yam suph* include Lake Ballah, Lake Timsah, Great Bitter Lake, and Little Bitter Lake. Due to the construction of the Suez Canal between the Gulf of Suez and the Mediterranean Sea, much of that area has changed, making it difficult to determine ancient locations today.

Whichever body of water, Scripture is clear that God miraculously allowed the Israelites to pass through the waters on dry ground, while destroying the Egyptian army as the waters crashed in.

Journey from Egypt to Mount Sinai

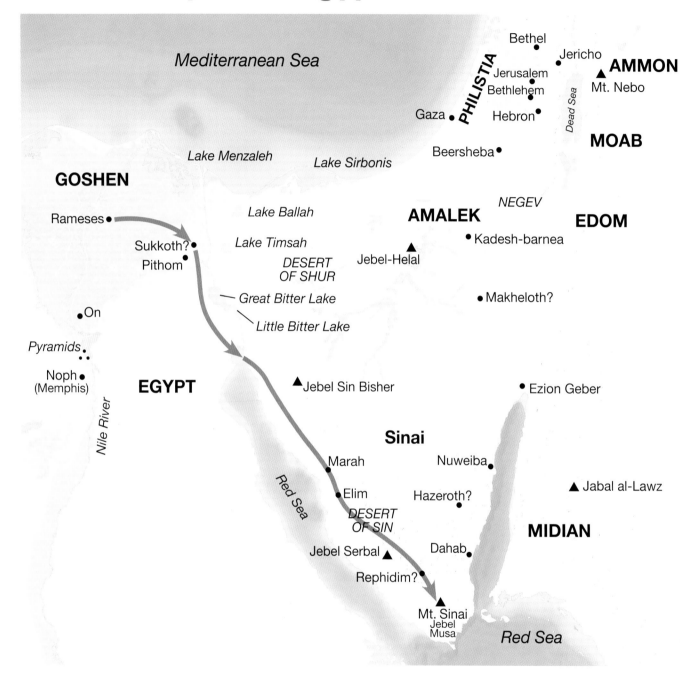

Southern Route

1. Israelites leave Egypt from Rameses and arrive in Sukkoth. Ex. 12:37

2. Israelites cross through the parted sea. Ex. 13:18; 14:29

3. God makes bitter water drinkable at Marah. Ex. 15:23–25

4. Israelites camp by palm trees and water at Elim. Ex. 15:27

5. God sends manna and quail in the Desert of Sin. Ex. 16:1–18

6. At Rephidim, God gives water from a rock and the Israelites defeat the Amalekites. Ex. 17:1–13

7. Israelites arrive at Mount Sinai. Ex. 19:1–2

At Mount Sinai

Exodus 19–40; Leviticus 1–27; Numbers 1–9

Moses and the Israelites spent about two years camped at the foot of Mount Sinai. What happens within this short period of time accounts for fifty-eight chapters of the Old Testament! Many of these chapters—including the entire book of Leviticus—consist of the instructions God gave his people about how to live as a "kingdom of priests and a holy nation" (Ex. 19:6).

At Sinai, God called Moses up to the mountain to meet with him. Moses became the mediator of a covenant between God and Israel. In a special way, Moses represented Israel to God and God to Israel. Through Moses, God gave the Ten Commandments (Ex. 20:2–17); detailed instructions for building the tabernacle and its furnishings, including the most sacred item, the ark of the covenant (Ex. 25:8, 22); and laws to govern the people's lives, worship practices, priesthood, and society.

"If you obey me fully and keep my covenant, then out of all nations you will be my treasured possession. Although the whole earth is mine, you will be for me a kingdom of priests and a holy nation." These are the words you are to speak to the Israelites. So Moses went back and summoned the elders of the people and set before them all the words the LORD had commanded him to speak. The people all responded together, "We will do everything the LORD has said." (Ex. 19:5–8)

The Mosaic covenant became a touchstone for Israel throughout biblical history.

For the Israelites, God's law was more than just following rules. It was about learning how to live with God in their midst. Observing these divine laws made it possible for a sinful people to dwell with a holy God. Once the tabernacle construction was complete, a thick cloud descended on the tent and "the glory of the LORD filled the tabernacle" (Ex. 40:34). This was visible confirmation for the people that God had done as he promised: "I will dwell among them" (Ex. 25:8).

After two years in the desert of Sinai, at the Lord's command, Moses and the Israelites to set out toward the promised land of Canaan (Num. 10:11–13).

THE ARK OF THE COVENANT ⟨⟨⟨

The ark was the first item of furniture constructed after God told Moses to build the tabernacle. It was made of acacia wood and covered with gold. It was topped with two winged cherubim facing each other. The ark contained three items: the tablets of the Ten Commandments, a jar of manna, and Aaron's staff. The ark was put in the most holy place of the tabernacle. Once a year, the high priest made atonement for sin at the ark on the Day of Atonement (Lev. 16). The top or the lid of the ark was called the mercy seat.

Moses descends from Mount Sinai with the Ten Commandments by Ferdinand Bol, 1662

The Wilderness Wanderings

Numbers 10–36; Deuteronomy 1–34

The Israelites continued to journey through the wilderness, far from the only home they had known in Egypt. They had left their lives of slavery in Egypt to follow God's promise to give them a new land. They had come so far from Egypt and witnessed the awesome power of God over Pharaoh and their oppressors, yet when it came time to take on the people in Canaan, their trust in God faltered.

Moses sent twelve spies into Canaan to explore the land. When the spies returned, ten advised the Israelites not to go in because it was too dangerous and the inhabitants too fierce. Only two, Caleb and Joshua, urged the people to trust God and enter the land. But the people listened to the ten instead: "All the Israelites grumbled against Moses and Aaron, and the whole assembly said to them, 'If only we had died in Egypt! Or in this wilderness!'" (Num. 14:2). They would've rather been back in Egypt, the land of their captivity! Though God didn't send them back to Egypt, he did give them their second request—to die in the wilderness. The Lord declared to Moses that this faithless generation would not enter the promised land (Num. 14:20–35).

The Israelites lived as nomads in the wilderness for forty years (counting from the year they left Egypt). Despite their disobedience to God, he still provided for them. God miraculously gave them food and water, and victory over their enemies. But he also sent judgment and plagues when they sinned to bring them back to obedience to the covenant made at Sinai. When they repented of their sins, he healed and restored them.

In time, Moses' sister, Miriam, passed away, as did Aaron the first high priest of Israel. At the end of the wilderness wanderings, the adults who emerged from Egypt in the exodus had died; their children, now grown, stood at the edge of the promised land in the plains of Moab. The book of Deuteronomy consists of Moses' speeches on these plains to this next generation. Moses urged them to remain faithful to their covenant with God: "Be careful that you do not forget the LORD, who brought you out of Egypt, out of the land of slavery" (Deut. 6:12).

Though God did not allow Moses to enter the promised land, he gave Moses a view of the land from Mount Nebo before Moses' death. Deuteronomy concludes with these words about Moses: "No prophet has risen in Israel like Moses, whom the LORD knew face to face, who did all those signs and wonders the LORD sent him to do in Egypt—to Pharaoh and to all his officials and to his whole land. For no one has ever shown the mighty power or performed the awesome deeds that Moses did in the sight of all Israel" (Deut. 34:10–12).

Exodus

Time/Place

The book of Exodus (which means "going out") begins almost three hundred years after Joseph's story. The book tells the story of how God, through Moses, led the descendants of Jacob (Israel) out of slavery in Egypt to Mount Sinai.

The Book

Exodus shows how God provided for and protected his people along their journey. The book closes with the Israelites at Sinai where God's glory fills the tabernacle, a sign God's presence.

Key Verse

"I am the LORD your God, who brought you out of Egypt, out of the land of slavery. You shall have no other gods before me" (Ex. 20:2–3).

Leviticus

Time/Place

The book of Leviticus takes place within the two years that the Israelites spent camped at the foot of Mount Sinai.

The Book

Leviticus is a series of divine directives about sacrifices, priestly duties, ritual purity, feasts of Israel, and holy ("set apart") living.

Though the book's name is derived from a Greek word *leyiticon* that means "things concerning the Levites," the instructions were not just for the Israelite tribe of Levi, but rather they were for the entire nation of Israel.

Key Verse

"Be holy, because I am holy" (Lev. 11:45).

Numbers

Time/Place

The book of Numbers narrates the years of wilderness wanderings after the Israelites left Mount Sinai.

The Book

The book is named *Numbers* because of the two censuses recorded in chapters 1 and 26. In Exodus, God had promised the Israelites that he would be with them on their way out of captivity. In Numbers, we see God remaining faithful to this promise despite his people's unfaithfulness and rebellion. The book ends with the Israelites camped in Moab just outside the promised land.

Key Verse

"The LORD is slow to anger, abounding in love and forgiving sin and rebellion. Yet he does not leave the guilty unpunished" (Num. 14:18).

Deuteronomy

Time/Place

The book of Deuteronomy takes place about forty years after the exodus on the plains of Moab at the edge of the promised land.

The Book

The book's name comes from the Greek word *deuteronomion* meaning "second law." Deuteronomy consists of encouraging and challenging speeches Moses gave to the next generation as they were about to enter Canaan. The book closes with Moses viewing the promised land from Mount Nebo just before his death. His successor Joshua would lead the Israelites into the land.

Key Verse

"Love the LORD your God with all your heart and with all your soul and with all your strength" (Deut. 6:5).

Feasts of Israel

In Leviticus 23, God established seven annual feasts to remind the people of the great things he had done for them: miracles, victories, and provision. These holy days were special times for God's people to meet with him.

"These are the LORD'S appointed festivals, the sacred assemblies you are to proclaim at their appointed times" (Lev. 23:4).

- ♦ Passover (Pesach)
- ♦ Unleavened Bread (Hag HaMatzot)
- ♦ Firstfruits (Reishit)
- ♦ Feasts of Weeks or Pentecost (Shavuot)
- ♦ Feast of Trumpets (Rosh HaShanah)
- ♦ Day of Atonement (Yom Kippur)
- ♦ Feast of Booths or Tabernacles (Sukkot)

Three of the seven appointed feasts were pilgrimage feasts when all Jewish males were required to go to Jerusalem to "appear before the LORD" (Deut. 16:16): the Feast of Unleavened Bread, the Feast of Weeks, and the Feast of Booths.

Two additional holidays developed much later in Jewish history:

- ♦ Feast of Lots (Purim) was established in the fifth century BC during the time of Queen Esther (Est. 9:20–32).
- ♦ Feast of Dedication (Hanukkah) was established in the second century BC, between the Old and New Testaments. (John 10:22 mentions Jesus being in Jerusalem during the Feast of Dedication.)

As the first Passover was about to happen, God also established the order of the months (Ex. 12:1–2). This was the first Jewish calendar used to determine the holidays (religious year). Passover is observed in the first month, Nisan, to remember the redemption of Israel from Egypt.

The Gregorian calendar used by most Western nations today is a solar calendar. The Jewish calendar uses both lunar and solar movements. The months are determined by the moon, and the year by the sun. The Jewish day begins at sunset.

After the Babylonian exile in the sixth century BC, the Jewish calendar reflected the Babylonian names of the months. These names still exist today in the Jewish religious calendar.

By the time of Jesus in the first century AD, there was a second calendar used for civil affairs. This calendar begins with the month of Tishri. The first of Tishri was the civil New Year, Rosh HaShanah. This calendar is still in use today.

Feasts of Israel

Feast	Scripture	Observed	Description
Passover Pesach	Ex. 12:1–13:16; Lev. 23:4–5	14 Nisan (March/April) In the first month of the religious year.	In the tenth plague on Egypt, the firstborn males of every house died unless the doorframe of that house was covered with the blood of a perfect lamb. The Lord "passed over" the homes with lamb's blood on the doorframes.
Unleavened Bread Hag HaMatzot	Ex. 12:15–20; Lev. 23:6–8	15–21 Nisan (March/April)	The Lord said that for seven days his people must eat unleavened bread (matzah). This bread was made in a hurry from flour and water without yeast to represent how the Lord brought the Israelites out of Egypt in haste.
Firstfruits Reishit	Lev. 23:9–14	16 Nisan (March/April) Third day after Passover.	A priest waved a sheaf of grain before the Lord as a firstfruits offering.
Feast of Weeks / Pentecost Shavuot	Lev. 23:15–22	6 Sivan (May/June) Fifty days after Passover.	This was a day to present an offering of new grain of the summer wheat harvest to the Lord. Pentecost means "fiftieth."
Feast of Trumpets Rosh HaShanah	Lev. 23:23–25	1 Tishri (September/October) Start of the High Holy Days.	This was a day of rest and food offerings commemorated with trumpet blasts. (Today, Rosh HaShanah begins the civil new year.)
Day of Atonement Yom Kippur	Lev. 23:26–32	10 Tishri (September/October) End of the High Holy Days.	On this holiest day of the year, the high priest entered the Most Holy Place of the tabernacle/temple where the ark was placed. He offered the blood of a sacrificed animal on the mercy seat of the ark to atone for the sins of Israel.
Feast of Booths Sukkot	Lev. 23:33–43	15–22 Tishri (September/October)	This week-long celebration of the fall harvest commemorates the forty-year wilderness journey. It was a time to build booths (temporary shelters) to remember how the Israelites lived under God's provision and protection in the wilderness.
Feast of Dedication Hanukkah	John 10:22; Also the book of Maccabees (Apocrypha)	25 Kislev–2 Tevet (November/December)	In the second century BC, the Maccabean Revolt against the Seleucids was successful and the temple in Jerusalem was cleansed and rededicated.
Feast of Lots Purim	Est. 9:20–32	14 or 15 Adar (February/March)	This festival remembers the foiled plot of Haman to kill all the Jews in King Xerxes' kingdom. It's a celebration of the deliverance of the Jews through Queen Esther.

Feasts of Israel Calendar

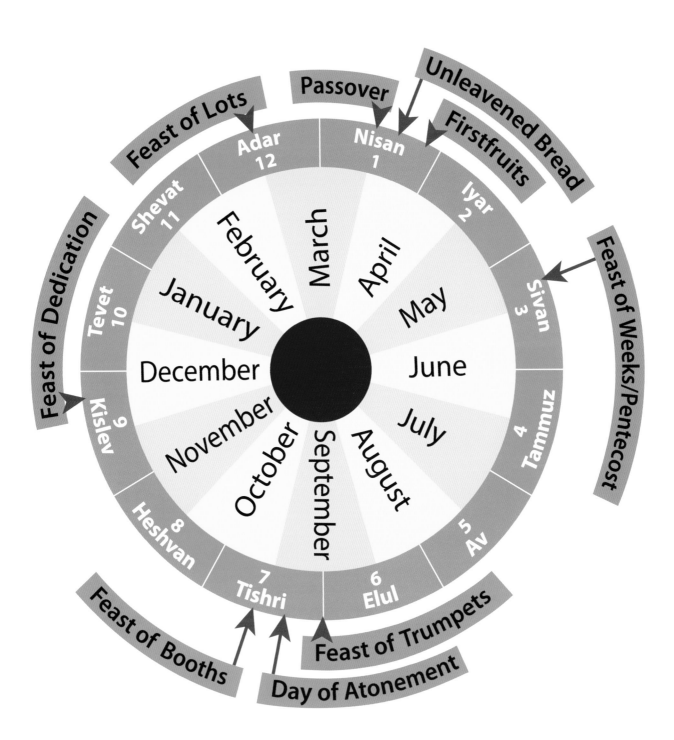

Chronology of the Ark of the Covenant

1. At Mount Sinai, Moses and the Israelites build the ark and place it in the tabernacle. Ex. 25; 40:1–33; 1446 BC

2. Israelites take the ark with them on their wilderness journey. Num. 4, 10, 14; Deut. 10

4. The tabernacle and ark are set up at Shiloh. Josh. 18:1

3. Priests carry the ark across the parted Jordan River as the Israelites enter Canaan. They carry it around Jericho for seven days and the city walls fall down. Josh. 3, 6; 1406 BC

5. The ark is taken to Bethel. Judg. 20:26–27

6. By the time of Samuel, the ark is back in Shiloh. 1 Sam. 3:3; 1100 BC

8. The ark is taken to Kiriath Jearim and remains there for 20 years. 1 Sam. 7:2

7. Philistines capture the ark but are forced to return it. 1 Sam. 4–6; 7:2

9. Saul brings the ark into battle against the Philistines. 1 Sam. 14:18

10. The ark stays at the house of Obed Edom for three months. 2 Sam. 6:10–11; 1 Chron. 13:6; 1004 BC

11. King David brings the ark to Jerusalem.

2 Sam. 6:1–15; 1004 BC

12. King Solomon builds the temple in Jerusalem and places the ark in the temple's Most Holy Place.

1 Kings 8:1–9; 2 Chron. 5:2–10; 960 BC

14. Jeremiah prophesies that one day "people will no longer say, 'The ark of the covenant of the Lord.' It will never enter their minds or be remembered; it will not be missed, nor will another one be made."

Jer. 3:16

13. By the time of King Josiah, the ark is no longer in the temple. Josiah discovers the book of the law and puts the ark back in the temple. (This is the last mention in the Bible of the ark's whereabouts.)

2 Chron. 35:3; 623 BC

15. Babylonians invade Jerusalem and burn the temple. It's believed the ark was either destroyed or carried off into Babylon with other sacred temple items.

2 Kings 25:13–17; 586 BC

16. The exiles return to Jerusalem and rebuild the temple, but there is no mention of the ark.

Ezra 4:11–12; 6:15; 516 BC

17. By the time of Jesus, there is still no ark in the temple. The last mention of the ark in the Bible is in John's vision of the temple of God in heaven.

Rev. 11:19

(Dates are approximate.)

Jacob's descendants (Hebrews/Israelites) live in Egypt for 430 years, part of that time in slavery.
Ex. 1

Moses is born.
Ex. 2:1–10

1526 BC

Moses flees to Midian.
Ex. 2:11–25

God speaks to Moses from a burning bush.
Ex. 3–4

1800 BC   1700 BC   1600 BC   1500 BC

The two Old Testament prophets who appeared at Jesus' Transfiguration were Elijah and Moses.
Matt. 17:2–3

God instructed Moses to go to the Israelites and tell them "I AM" (Yahweh/YHWH) had sent Moses. Jesus used this same designation ("I am" and "I am who I am") to refer to himself.
Ex. 3:13–15; John 8:24, 58; 13:19

God parts the sea.
Ex. 14

Songs of Moses and Miriam.
Ex. 15:1–21

God turns bitter water into drinkable water.
Ex. 15:22–27

God sends manna and quail.
Ex. 16

Moses strikes a rock and water flows from it.
Ex. 17:1–7

Jesus declared that he is the true bread that came down from heaven: "Your ancestors ate manna and died, but whoever feeds on this bread will live forever." John 6:58

TIME LINE KEY

 Prophecy Fulfilled by Jesus

 Person in the Genealogy of Jesus

 New Testament Connection

Dates are approximate.

This time line follows a "high date" of the exodus at 1446 BC. For a "low date" of 1290 BC, the dates for events following the exodus (Passover, Mount Sinai, etc.) would begin 156 years later, placing Moses' death at 1250 BC.

Moses confronts Pharaoh in Egypt.
Ex. 5–6

God sends 10 plagues on Egypt.
Ex. 7–12

First Passover
Ex. 12:1–30

Exodus: Israelites leave Egypt.
Ex. 12:31–42

1446 BC

God leads Israelites with pillars of cloud and fire.
Ex. 13:21–22

✝ John the Baptist identified Jesus as the "Lamb of God, who takes away the sin of the world!" The apostle Paul called Jesus "our Passover lamb."
John 1:29; 1 Cor. 5:7

✝ One requirement for the Passover lamb was that it have no broken bones. When Jesus was crucified on the cross his bones remained unbroken Ex. 12:46; Num. 9:12; John 19:31–36

Israelites defeat the Amalekites.
Ex. 17:8–16

Moses' father-in-law, wife, and sons go to him in the wilderness.
Ex. 18

Mosaic Covenant: God gives the Ten Commandments/ Law and tabernacle instructions at Mount Sinai.
Ex. 19–31

Aaron constructs a golden calf idol.
Ex. 32

Moses sees God's "back."
Ex. 33–34

📖 As the giving of the law marked the beginning of the Mosaic covenant, the giving of the Holy Spirit at Pentecost confirmed the new covenant initiated by Jesus. Acts 2

✝ In the Sermon on the Mount, Jesus said, "Do not think that I have come to abolish the Law or the Prophets; I have not come to abolish them but to fulfill them." Matt. 5:17

45

Tabernacle and ark of the covenant built.
Ex. 35–40

First census
Num. 1

Instructions for holy living.
Lev. 1–27;
Num. 2–9

Israelites leave Mount Sinai.
Num. 10

1444 BC

God sends fire, quail, and plague.
Num. 11

The book of Hebrews explains that the things of the Old Covenant—tabernacle, sacrifices, law—were "shadows" of the good things to come. The temporary things of earth pointed toward the eternal things of heaven.
Heb. 8:5; 9:23–24; 10:1

Jesus said that "all the Law and the Prophets hang on" two commandments: "Love the Lord your God with all your heart and with all your soul and with all your mind" and "Love your neighbor as yourself."
Lev. 19:18; Deut. 6:5; Matt. 22:34–40

Miriam dies.
Num. 20

Moses strikes a rock instead of speaking to it as God instructed.
Num. 20

Aaron dies.
Num. 20

People healed by looking up at a bronze snake.
Num. 21

Israelite victories.
Num. 21

Israelites camp at Moab; Balaam's blessings.
Num. 22

Jesus explained to Nicodemus: "Just as Moses lifted up the snake in the wilderness, so the Son of Man must be lifted up, that everyone who believes may have eternal life in him." John 3:14–15

Miriam punished with leprosy but restored.
Num. 12

The twelve spies explore Canaan.
Num. 13

The Israelites refuse to enter Canaan.
Num. 14

Instructions for offerings and Sabbath.
Num. 15

Rebellion and death in the camp.
Num. 16

Instructions for Aaron, priests, and Levites.
Num. 17–19

Aaron was the first high priest of Israel, but Jesus is the eternal High Priest of all humankind: ". . . a merciful and faithful high priest in service to God, and that he might make atonement for the sins of the people."
Heb. 2:17; 4:15

Second census
Num. 26

Instructions for the tribes of Israel.
Num. 27–36

Moses' speeches on the plains of Moab.
Deut. 1–33

Moses views the promised land from Mount Nebo.
Deut. 34:1–4

Moses dies at 120 years old.
Deut. 34:5–12

1406 BC

1400 BC

God promised to one day raise up a prophet like Moses, speaking God's words. When Jesus came, many recognized him as this prophet. Deut. 18:15–19; John 1:45; 6:14; 7:40; Acts 3:18–22

CHAPTER 4

The Land of Promise

From Joshua to the Judges
1400–1100 BC

Conquest of Canaan

The Judges of Israel

The Story of Ruth

Joshua had been one of the two spies who returned from the promised land with a favorable report for Moses. The other ten spies had persuaded the Israelites to stay out, for people who lived in the land were big and powerful, like giants in their eyes. Joshua, however, challenged the Israelites to have courage: "The LORD is with us. Do not be afraid" (Num. 14:9). But the people listened to their fears more than God's promises. As a result, God let them wander in the wilderness until that generation passed away.

Fast-forward almost forty years, and Joshua again stood at the edge of the promised land. God had given his people another chance to find the courage that the earlier generation lacked—this time, to take on the giants in the land.

Conquest of Canaan

Joshua 1–24

Joshua was Moses' appointed successor to lead the Israelites into Canaan (Num. 27:18–20). Like Moses, Joshua had a promise from God: "I will never leave you nor forsake you" (Josh. 1:5).

The entry into the land began with a miraculous sign of God's presence. God parted the Jordan River so the people entered across dry land. This was reminiscent of the Red Sea parting as Moses and the Israelites left Egypt. The conquest of cities in Canaan began with God tumbling the massive walls of Jericho. Rahab, a Canaanite woman in Jericho who wisely understood what was happening, said, "I know that the LORD has given you this land.

. . . For the LORD your God is God in heaven above and earth below" (Josh. 2:9, 11). When Jericho fell, she and her family were spared because of her faith and assistance to Israel.

Then, Joshua and his army moved through central Canaan. Near Shechem, between Mount Ebal and Mount Gerizim, Joshua and all the people assembled to worship the Lord (Josh. 8:34; see also Deut. 11:29). Shechem was the location where Abraham and his family had settled centuries earlier when God called him to move to Canaan (Gen. 12:6). Joshua built an altar on Mount Ebal, the priests presented offerings to the Lord, and Joshua read the law of Moses to all the people, reminding them to obey their covenant with God.

Next, Joshua conquered cities in the southern region of Canaan, followed by victories in the north. In all these battles, God was their behind-the-scenes military commander, present and empowering (Josh. 5:13–15). Feared by the people of the land, the Israelites quickly settled throughout Canaan and Joshua allotted specific territories to the different tribes of Israel.

The book closes with Joshua's farewell address in which he reminds the people to remain faithful to God as God was faithful to them. Joshua memorably declared:

> "Choose for yourselves this day whom you will serve, whether the gods your ancestors served beyond the Euphrates, or the gods of the Amorites, in whose land you are living. But as for me and my household, we will serve the LORD." (Josh. 24:15)

Joshua died at 110 years old and was buried in the promised land.

Joshua's Route of Conquest

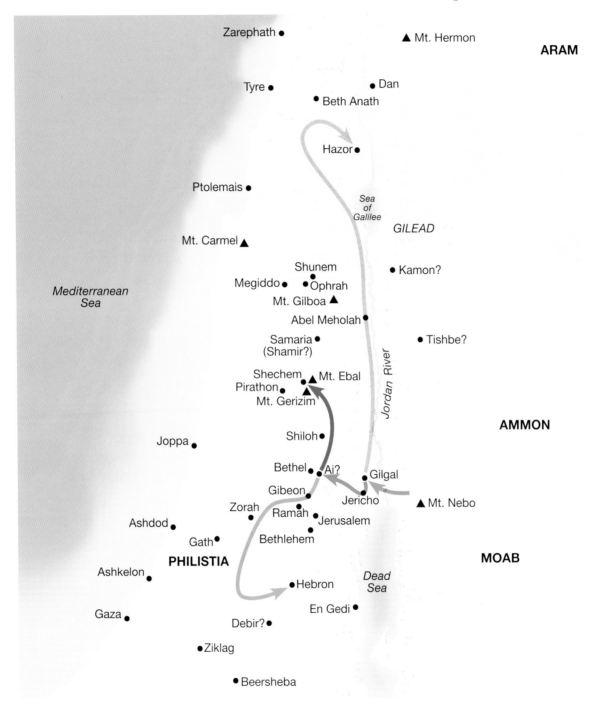

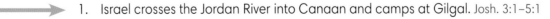

1. Israel crosses the Jordan River into Canaan and camps at Gilgal. Josh. 3:1–5:1

2. Central conquest: Jericho and Ai. Josh. 6:1–27; 8:1–29

3. Israel renews the covenant between Mount Ebal and Mount Gerizim. Josh 8:30–34

4. Southern conquest: Gibeon, Hebron, and other cities. Josh. 9:1–10:43

5. Northern conquest: Hazor and other cities. Josh. 11:1–23

The Judges

Judges 1–21

Joshua's death left the tribes of Israel without a central leader. The Lord was supposed to be their King, but as we read at the beginning of the book of Judges, "another generation grew up who knew neither the LORD nor what he had done for Israel" (Judg. 2:10). Moses had told the people, "Remember the LORD your God," but this new generation soon forgot (Deut. 8:18). The awesome victories of the past became distant, forgotten tales.

The book of Judges portrays repeated cycles of sin and deliverance during this era.

Sin: Though Israel had conquered many key cities in Canaan, they settled alongside the remaining Canaanites in the land (Judg. 2:20–23). In ancient Near East religions, people believed that a multitude of deities ruled over all aspects of life. In Canaan, the goddess Ashtaroth and the god Baal were believed to grant worshipers fertility in humans and animals and rain for crops. The Israelites often turned to these false gods instead of trusting in the one true God to provide for their needs.

Oppression: In response to Israel's sins, God allowed other nations to oppress Israel. This oppression wasn't a mere inconvenience; in the ancient world, it was brutal and violent. Many Israelites probably felt like the farmer Gideon when he said, "Where are all [God's] wonders that our ancestors told us about? . . . The LORD has abandoned us" (Judg. 6:13).

Repentance: In desperation, the Israelites eventually cried out to God: "We have sinned against you, forsaking our God and serving the Baals" (Judg. 10:10).

Deliverance: In his mercy, God raised up a leader (a "judge") to deliver Israel from their oppressors. Notable among the twelve judges in the book of Judges are Deborah, Gideon, and Samson. Deborah was a prophetess who led Israel to defeat King Jabin who "cruelly oppressed the Israelites for twenty years" (Judg. 4:3). Gideon, an ordinary farmer and "least" among his family, was called by God to lead extraordinary military victories (Judg. 6:15). Samson was a foolish and revengeful man whom God, nevertheless, empowered with amazing physical strength to accomplish God's purpose of breaking Philistine dominance over Israel (Judg. 16:31).

Peace: With the success of each judge, Israel experienced a time of peace. But eventually Israel fell back into worshiping other gods, and the cycle would start again.

Interestingly, the last five chapters in the book of Judges don't include any judges. This section consists of stories about Israelite violence, idolatry, and civil war between the tribes of Israel. In addition to outside oppressors, the people of God were oppressing each other too! Why was everything so chaotic? These chapters explain, "In those days, Israel had no king and everyone did as they saw fit" (Judg. 17:6; 18:1; 21:25).

Samson by Joaquín Espalter y Rull, c. 1850

Cycle in the Book of Judges

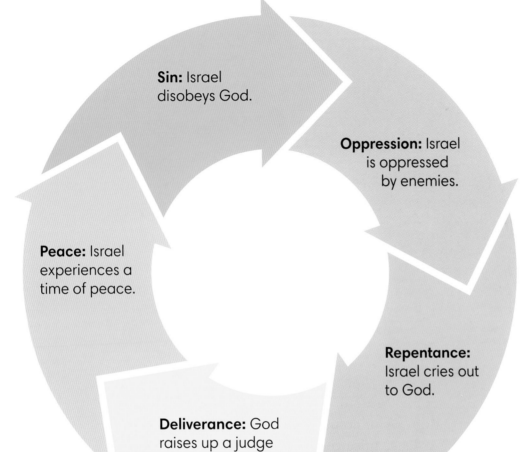

Sin: Israel disobeys God.

Oppression: Israel is oppressed by enemies.

Peace: Israel experiences a time of peace.

Repentance: Israel cries out to God.

Deliverance: God raises up a judge to deliver Israel.

The Judges

Judge and Meaning of Name	Scripture	Location	Enemy	Years of Oppression	Years of Peace
Othniel Lion of God	Judg. 1:12–14; 3:7–11	Debir	Mesopotamians	8	40
Ehud Strong	Judg. 3:12–30	Gilgal	Moabites	18	80
Shamgar Cupbearer	Judg. 3:31	Possibly Beth Anath	Philistines	Unknown	Unknown
Deborah Bee	Judg. 4:1–5:31	Between Bethel and Ramah	Canaanites	20	40
Gideon A cutting down	Judg. 6:1–8:32	Ophrah	Midianites	7	40
Tola Scarlet	Judg. 10:1–2	Shamir	Unknown	Unknown	23
Jair The Lord enlightens	Judg. 10:3–5	Kamon in Gilead	Unknown	Unknown	22
Jephthah He opens	Judg. 10:6–12:7	Gilead	Philistines; Ammonites	18	6
Ibzan Splendid	Judg. 12:8–10	Bethlehem	Unknown	Unknown	7
Elon Oak	Judg. 12:11–12	Zebulun	Unknown	Unknown	10
Abdon Service	Judg. 12:13–15	Pirathon	Unknown	Unknown	8
Samson Distinguished or sun	Judg. 13:1–16:31	Zorah	Philistines	40	20

Years of oppression refer to the times God allowed Israel to be dominated by enemies. Years of peace refer to the times when God raised up a judge. It's important to note, however, that the stories of the judges occurred in different places and the time frames of some judges probably overlapped. Also, some numbers might be estimates or symbolic. For example, forty years often means one generation, not forty years exactly. This makes the chronology of the book difficult to pinpoint.

Life of Samson

God's Activity	Samson's Activity	Event	Scripture
God Intervenes	Is Born	By God's intervention, Samson is born to an infertile couple at a time when the Philistines oppressed Israel. Samson is given the Nazirite vow (no wine, no contact with the dead, no cutting his hair).	Judg. 13:1–25
God Moves	Gets Married	Samson falls in love with a Philistine woman and marries her. God moved him to marry her to cause a confrontation with the Philistines.	Judg. 14:1–4
God Empowers	Kills a Lion	Samson kills a lion with his bare hands. Later, he takes honey from the carcass, a violation of his Nazirite vow.	Judg. 14:5–9
God Empowers	Gets Revenge	Samson kills thirty Philistine men as retribution for the Philistines forcing his wife to betray him.	Judg. 14:10–20
God Allows	Gets Revenge	Samson uses foxes and fire to destroy the Philistines' fields after his wife is given in marriage to another man.	Judg. 15:1–8
God Empowers	Kills His Captors	Samson flees to Judah, where he is bound and handed over to the Philistines. He breaks loose and kills 1,000 Philistines using a donkey's jawbone.	Judg. 15:9–17
God Provides	Prays	Samson thinks he will die of thirst and prays to God. The Lord provides water for him.	Judg. 15:18–20
God Is Silent	Escapes and Demonstrates His Strength	After spending the night with a prostitute in a Philistine city, Samson escapes from the men of the city who plot to kill him. In a show of strength, he removes the doors of the city gate.	Judg. 16:1–3
God Is Silent	Falls in Love	Samson falls for another Philistine woman—Delilah.	Judg. 16:4
God Is Silent	Is Fooled and Captured	After three separate attempts, Delilah gets Samson to reveal the secret of his strength. She cuts his hair, weakening him, and the Philistines easily capture him.	Judg. 16:5–22
God Empowers	Prays and Ends His Life	While enslaved and humiliated at a Philistine temple, Samson prays to God. The Lord strengthens him and Samson pushes down the pillars of the temple, killing himself and many Philistines.	Judg. 16:23–31

▶▶▶ GOD'S JUDGMENT

The reasons for the conquest in the book of Joshua are best viewed in light of other Old Testament passages. For example, Moses explained to Israel: "Do not say to yourself, 'The LORD has brought me here to take possession of this land because of my righteousness.' No, it is on account of the wickedness of these nations that the LORD is going to drive them out before you" (Deut. 9:5). From this perspective, God used Israel as a means to bring judgment upon wicked nations (Gen. 15:16; Lev. 18:24.) Yet God also sometimes used other nations to execute his judgment upon Israel when they did evil (2 Kings 18:9–12; Judg. 2:11–15).

Joshua

Time/Place
The book of Joshua covers the years after Moses' death when Joshua led the Israelites into the promised land. The conquest of Canaan is estimated to have taken about seven years.

The Book
Chapters 1–12 cover Joshua's conquest of Canaan, and chapters 13–22 explain the allotment of the land among the tribes of Israel. Chapters 23–24 are Joshua's farewell.

Key Verse
"Be strong and courageous. Do not be afraid; do not be discouraged, for the LORD your God will be with you wherever you go" (Josh. 1:9).

Judges

Time/Place
The book of Judges takes place in Canaan during the era between Joshua and Samuel.

The Book
The first two chapters of Judges explain how the conquest of Canaan was incomplete. Chapters 3–16 tell the stories of twelve judges of Israel. The final chapters, 17–21, describe a time of sin and strife among the tribes of Israel.

Key Verse
"Whenever the LORD raised up a judge for them, he was with the judge and saved them out of the hands of their enemies as long as the judge lived" (Judg. 2:18).

Ruth

Time/Place
The book of Ruth takes place in Bethlehem (and for a short time in Moab) during the latter part of the era of the judges.

The Book
The story is about Naomi, a widow who had lost all hope; her daughter-in-law Ruth, a faithful foreigner; Boaz, a compassionate guardian-redeemer; but mostly, it's about the God who restored their lives with joy.

Key Verse
"But Ruth replied, 'Don't urge me to leave you or to turn back from you. Where you go I will go, and where you stay I will stay. Your people will be my people and your God my God'" (Ruth 1:16).

The Story of Ruth

The book of Ruth is set during a latter part of the era of the judges, a time when Israel's spiritual and social life was a mess (Ruth 1:1). (Read the last five chapters in the book of Judges to get an idea of how chaotic life was at that time.) Ruth's story is quite different than the stories in the book of Judges. Ruth's story doesn't include amazing feats of strength like in Samson's story or shocking military victories like in Gideon's; but to the two widowed women in this story, what God did in their lives must have seemed just as miraculous.

This story begins with a famine that caused Naomi and her family to move from Bethlehem to Moab. (Moab had been an enemy of Israel; see Judges 3:12). Naomi's husband and her two sons died in Moab. In ancient Near East culture, women were only valued by their connection to a man, so Naomi's circumstances left her destitute. She returned to Bethlehem, but she was not alone. Naomi's daughter-in-law, Ruth, a Moabitess and also a widow, chose to go with her. Ruth pledged loyalty to Naomi: "Where you go I will go, and where you stay I will stay. Your people will be my people and your God my God" (Ruth 1:16). Life in Bethlehem would not be any easier for Ruth. She was a widow, childless, and a foreigner.

In Bethlehem, Ruth worked among the poor, gleaning leftovers in grain fields. But God was at work behind the scenes of her life. The field she gleaned in belonged to an Israelite named Boaz. He had heard of Ruth's unwavering dedication to Naomi, and he was moved to compassion toward Ruth.

By the end of the story, Boaz, an Israelite and "a man of worth" (Ruth 2:1), is married to Ruth, a Moabitess and "a woman of noble character" (Ruth 3:11). Being from the same clan as Naomi's family, Boaz acted as a "guardian-redeemer" (Ruth 2:20) and bought back Naomi's family land for her. The Lord blessed Ruth and Boaz with a son—a grandson for Naomi who renewed her life with joy (Ruth 4:15). It's from this child's lineage that King David and, most importantly, Jesus the Messiah would come (Matt. 1:5–6).

God's love shines through this story in the lives of ordinary people who showed extraordinary kindness and loyalty during a time when those qualities were difficult to find.

NAMES IN THE BOOK OF RUTH

Bethlehem means "house of bread," which Naomi's family leaves, ironically because of a famine. Naomi means "pleasant," but after suffering the loss of her husband and sons, she changes her name to Mara, meaning "bitterness." Naomi's two sons who die in Moab are named Mahlon and Kilion, which mean "sickly" and "weakly." Ruth means "friend" or "companion." Boaz may mean "lively" or "strength."

Ruth in Boaz's Field by Julius Schnorr von Carolsfeld, 1828

Joshua succeeds Moses as Israel's leader. Josh. 1

1406 BC

Israelites spy out the land. Rahab hides the spies. Josh. 2

God parts the Jordan River and the Israelites walk through on dry land. Josh. 3–5

Israelites march around Jericho 7 days, walls collapse, and the city is conquered. Rahab and her family are spared. Josh. 6

1400 BC

Jesus is the Greek form of the name *Yeshua* or *Joshua* which means "the Lord saves."

Rahab is listed in Jesus' genealogy. Matt. 1:5

Rahab is described as a hero of faith and righteousness. Heb. 11:31; James 2:25

When Jesus entered Jericho, he made it a place of healing: blind Bartimaeus received sight and Zacchaeus spiritual healing. Mark 10:46–52; Luke 18:35–43; 19:1–9

Israel renews the covenant; Joshua's farewell. Josh. 23–24

Joshua dies at 110 years old. Josh. 24:29–33

Israel forsakes God. Then, judges Othniel, Ehud, and Shamgar lead Israel. Judg. 1–3

Judge Deborah and military leader Barak defeat their oppressors. Jael kills an enemy commander with a tent peg. Judg. 4–5

Judge Gideon defeats the Midianites. Judg. 6–8

1300 BC

Barak and Gideon are listed as heroes of faith. Heb. 11:32

TIME LINE KEY

 Prophecy Fulfilled by Jesus

 Person in the Genealogy of Jesus

 New Testament Connection

Chronology of the judges is uncertain. They are listed here in the order they appear in the book of Judges.

Dates are approximate.

Achan disobeys God, so it takes two attempts to defeat the city of Ai.
Josh. 7–8

Israel renews the covenant at Mounts Ebal and Gerizim.
Josh. 8:30–35

Gibeonites trick Joshua into making a peace treaty with them.
Josh. 9

Joshua defeats cities in the south, then the north.
Josh. 10–12

Joshua divides the land among the tribes of Israel.
Josh. 13–22

The book of Hebrews explains that when Jesus came, he introduced "a better hope" because he became "the guarantor of a better covenant."
Heb. 7:18–22

As Joshua led God's people into rest in the promised land, Jesus leads his followers into rest in the new creation. Josh. 21:44;
Heb. 4:1–11

Gideon's son Abimelek kills his 70 brothers. In the end, he is killed by woman who drops a millstone on his head.
Judg. 9

Judges Tola, Jair, Jephthah, Ibzan, Elon, and Abdon lead Israel.
Judg. 10–12

Judge Samson fights the Philistines with incredible physical strength.
Judg. 13–16

Idolatry, violence, and war among the tribes of Israel.
Judg. 17–21

Ruth marries Boaz and has a child, an ancestor of King David.
Ruth 1–4

1200 BC

1100 BC

Jephthah and Samson are listed as heroes of the faith.
Heb. 11:32

Boaz and Ruth are listed in Jesus' genealogy. Matt. 1:5;
Luke 3:32

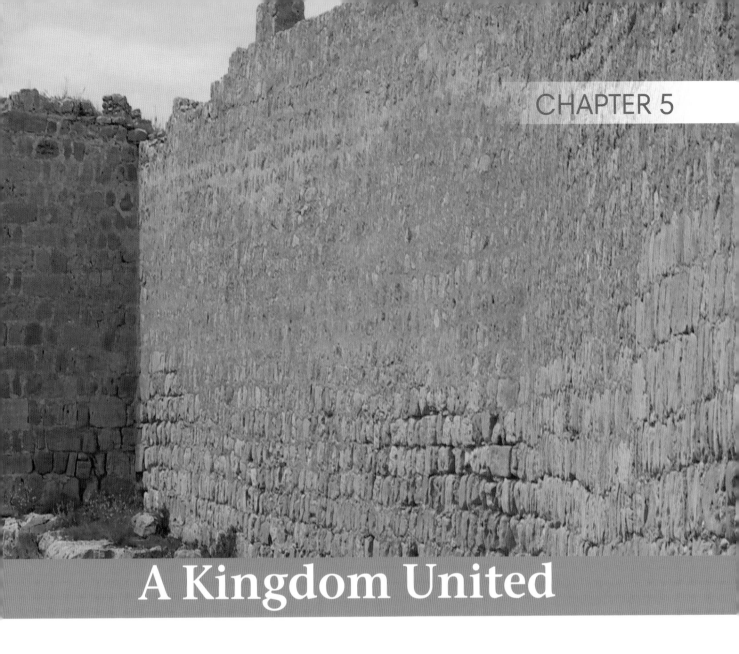

CHAPTER 5

A Kingdom United

From Samuel to Solomon
1100–950 BC

Kings Saul, David, and Solomon

Psalms to Song of Songs

Books of Samuel, Kings, and Chronicles

This story begins with a silent prayer from the heart of a woman in pain. Hannah had no children, which in the ancient world was considered a cause for ridicule and shame. "In her deep anguish Hannah prayed to the LORD, weeping bitterly" (1 Sam. 1:10). Her prayer was inaudible—a prayer from the depths of her heart. Those around her couldn't hear her, but the Lord did. He granted Hannah, as the psalmist would say, the "desires of [her] heart" (Ps. 37:4). Hannah conceived a son. She dedicated him to the Lord's service and named him Samuel, which in Hebrew sounds similar to "heard by God."

When Samuel was a young boy serving in the house of God, he heard the Lord's voice calling him, "Samuel! Samuel!" (1 Sam. 3:10). He was given a message from God, like great prophets before him.

The Lord heard Hannah's prayer and the boy Samuel heard the voice of God, but the question that looms over this era of biblical history is this: Will the people of Israel hear the voice of God and turn their hearts to him?

Samuel Relating to Eli the Judgements of God upon Eli's House by John Singleton Copley, 1780

Samuel, Saul, and David

1 Samuel 1–31; 1 Chronicles 1–10

Samuel led Israel both as a prophet and the last judge of the era of judges. Late in his life, the Israelites made it clear that they didn't want another judge to succeed him. They demanded a king like other nations. God explained to Samuel, "It is not you they have rejected, but they have rejected me as their king" (1 Sam. 8:7). The kingless era of judges was a difficult time when the tribes of Israel rarely looked to God as their King and instead turned to idols. Though God warned the Israelites that having a king would come with many unpleasant strings attached, the people insisted. So God instructed Samuel to anoint a man named Saul as Israel's first king.

Saul was handsome, young, and tall. He looked the part of a king. "The Spirit of God came powerfully upon [Saul]" and the people shouted, "Long live the king!" (1 Sam. 10:10, 24). Though Saul had initial successes as king, in time, he disobeyed the word of the Lord and ignored God's instructions. This prompted Samuel to declare a fateful prophecy: "Your kingdom will not endure; the LORD has sought out a man after his own heart" (1 Sam. 13:14). Another king would be chosen.

David was the youngest of eight brothers, a teenager who was given the chore of tending sheep. When God sent Samuel to David's family in Bethlehem, Samuel thought that surely the eldest brother—the tall one—would be Israel's next king. But as it turned out, God had chosen the youngest son, David the shepherd. (The Hebrew word for *youngest* in 1 Samuel 16:11 also means *smallest*.) "The LORD does not look at the things people look at. People look at the outward appearance, but the LORD looks at the heart" (1 Sam. 16:7). God had called David to leave the pastures of sheep to go shepherd the people of Israel. Centuries later, Jesus would call ordinary fishermen with willing hearts to leave their nets behind and go become disciples who fish for people (Matt. 4:18–22).

Once anointed by Samuel, the Spirit of the Lord came upon David and departed from Saul (1 Sam. 16:13–14).

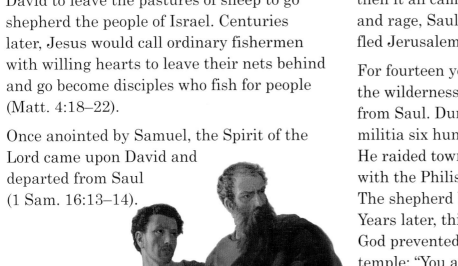

David quickly rose to prominence in Israel. He defeated a giant Philistine warrior Goliath with a simple slingshot. He forged an unbreakable friendship with Saul's son Jonathan, the heir apparent. He even married the king's daughter Michal. But then it all came tumbling down. In jealousy and rage, Saul nearly killed David, so David fled Jerusalem.

For fourteen years, David moved throughout the wilderness of Judah, living as a fugitive from Saul. During this time, David built up a militia six hundred men strong (1 Sam. 27:2). He raided towns and even lived for a time with the Philistines—the enemy of Israel! The shepherd boy had become a man of war. Years later, this would be cited as a reason God prevented David from building the temple: "You are not to build a house for my Name, because you have shed much blood on the earth in my sight" (1 Chron. 22:8).

Saul and his sons, including Jonathan, died in a battle against the Philistines. This put David in a position to take hold of the kingship for which God had anointed him years before.

After David mourned Saul's and Jonathan's deaths, he sought the Lord, asking, "Where shall I go?" "To Hebron," the Lord answered (2 Sam. 2:1). And David, a man after God's own heart, listened and obeyed.

Death of King Saul by Elie Marcuse, 1848

David's Journey from Shepherd to King

1. Samuel anoints David in Bethlehem. 1 Sam. 16:1–13

2. David kills Goliath in the Valley of Elah near Gath. 1 Sam. 17:2–53

3. David spends 14 years in the wilderness as a fugitive from King Saul. Key places include Gath (1 Sam. 21:10), En Gedi (1 Sam. 23:29), Philistia (1 Sam. 27:1), and Ziklag (1 Sam. 30:1).

4. Saul and Jonathan die in battle with the Philistines on Mount Gilboa. 1 Sam. 31:1–6

5. David is made king of Judah and reigns 7 ½ years from Hebron. 2 Sam. 2:4

6. David is made king of Israel and designates Jerusalem as the capital. He reigns for a total of 40 years. 2 Sam. 5:6–9; 1 Kings 2:10–11

King David

2 Samuel 1–24; 1 Chronicles 11–29; 1 Kings 1–2

In Hebron, David was made king over Judah and he ruled from there seven and a half years. Then the rest of the tribes made David king over all of Israel. David's first act as king of Israel was to make Jerusalem the national capital and bring the ark of the covenant into the city—a sign of God's power and presence. When the ark entered Jerusalem to the sound of trumpets and cheering, David was "dancing before the LORD with all his might" in celebratory abandon (2 Sam. 6:14). Almost half of the 150 psalms in the book of Psalms are attributed to David. These psalms reveal a man unhindered in expressing his heart's joyful praise, his thankfulness for God's goodness, but also his deep sorrow in times of suffering.

God blessed King David and gave him "rest from all his enemies" (2 Sam. 7:1). God also made a covenant with David: "Your kingdom will endure forever. . . . Your throne will be established forever" (2 Sam. 7:16). David brought national unity that Saul was not able to achieve between the warring tribes.

But at the height of his success, the king made a foolish choice. In secret, King David slept with Bathsheba, the wife of Uriah, one of David's elite military leaders (2 Sam. 11:3; 23:39). When Bathsheba got pregnant, David tried to conceal his sin by ensuring Uriah's death on the battlefield and marrying Bathsheba himself. But King David couldn't hide his sin from the King of Kings. God confronted David through the prophet Nathan, and David confessed that he, the man appointed by God to shepherd Israel, had abused his flock (2 Sam. 12:13). David's prayer for mercy is captured beautifully in Psalm 51:

> Create in me a pure heart, O God, and renew a steadfast spirit within me. Do not cast me from your presence or take your Holy Spirit from me. Restore to me the joy of your salvation and grant me a willing spirit, to sustain me. (Ps. 51:10–12)

David received forgiveness from God, but the consequences of his failure affected his family and kingdom. David's story in the book of 2 Samuel from this point on is a

THE DAVIDIC COVENANT ◀◀◀

God made a covenant with David promising that David's "kingdom will endure forever" and his "throne will be established forever" (2 Sam. 7:16). God used David's royal lineage to bring about the Messiah, Jesus Christ, who reigns eternally over the kingdom of God (Luke 1:32–33).

King David by Guercino, 1651

series of troubles. One of his sons assaulted his daughter (chapter 13). Another son, Absalom, attempted to usurp the throne and declare himself king (chapter 15). Disloyal leaders in David's kingdom attempted yet another coup (chapter 20). War between Israel and the Philistines resumed (chapter 21). A plague caused thousands in Israel to die (chapter 24).

David ruled Israel for forty years. Some of his last words were to his son Solomon who inherited the throne. Spoken from years of personal experience, David told his son, "Serve [the Lord] with wholehearted devotion and with a willing mind, for the LORD searches every heart and understands every desire and every thought" (1 Chron. 28:9).

King Solomon

2 Chronicles 1–9; 1 Kings 3–11

King Solomon reigned during the golden age of Israel, a time of national and economic prosperity. Solomon began his kingship by asking God for one thing: wisdom. He, like his father David, desired to govern God's people with "a discerning heart" (1 Kings 3:9). "God gave Solomon wisdom and very great insight, and a breadth of understanding as measureless as the sand on the seashores" (1 Kings 4:29). During Solomon's reign, he expanded the boundaries of Israel, achieved economic successes, constructed a magnificent palace, built the first temple in Jerusalem, and placed the ark of the covenant in the most holy room of the temple.

Solomon's wisdom is recorded in the books of Proverbs, Ecclesiastes, Song of Songs, and even two psalms (72, 127). First Kings

4:32 says that by the end of his life, Solomon had spoken over 3,000 proverbs and written 1,005 songs!

But wise advice is often easier given than taken. King Solomon married over 700 foreign wives and had 300 concubines. Royal marriages like this in the ancient world were a way of forming political and economic alliances between nations. Solomon may have seen his many marriages as a means to strengthen his kingdom, but in the end, this proved to be a foolish path to follow. As one of Solomon's own proverbs says, "There is a way that seems right to a man, but its end is the way of death" (Prov. 14:12 NKJV). In his old age, Solomon set up numerous places of worship for the gods of his many wives and his heart turned toward these idols. No longer was his heart "fully devoted to the LORD his God" (1 Kings 11:4). As Moses had said centuries earlier and Jesus would say centuries later, the greatest commandment is to "Love the Lord your God with all your heart and with all your soul and with all your mind" (Deut. 6:5; Matt. 22:37).

During most of Solomon's reign, Israel was united and prosperous. Upon his death, however, Solomon left behind a fragile kingdom on the verge of breaking apart.

Building of the Temple of Salomon by Santi di Tito, 1570

Psalms

Time/Place
The psalms were collected from as early as the time of David, around 1000 BC, to as late as Ezra, around 450 BC.

The Book
Psalms is a collection of 150 Hebrew songs, prayers, and poems. The psalms are expressions of joyful praise, cries of a heart in pain, thanksgiving for God's goodness, and teachings about who God is and what he has done. At least 73 psalms are attributed to David and two to Solomon.

Key Verses
"The LORD is my shepherd, I shall not want" (Ps. 23:1 KJV). "I have hidden your word in my heart" (Ps. 119:11). "Create in me a pure heart, O God" (Ps. 51:10).

Proverbs

Time/Place
Proverbs was compiled over a time span of about 900–700 BC.

The Book
Proverbs is a collection of memorable sayings that communicate observations about the world to help us live wise and godly lives. Most of the book was written by Solomon (Prov. 1:1; 10:1; 25:1), but other authors also contributed (Prov. 22:17; 24:23; 30:1; 31:1).

Key Verses
"The fear of the LORD is the beginning of knowledge" (Prov. 1:7). "Trust in the LORD with all your heart and lean not on your own understanding" (Prov. 3:5). "As iron sharpens iron, so one person sharpens another" (Prov. 27:17).

Ecclesiastes

Time/Place
Ecclesiastes (which means "the teacher") is anonymous, but the traditional view is that Solomon authored this book late in life.

The Book
Ecclesiastes is one of the most philosophical books of the Bible.

The author ponders the meaning—or apparent meaninglessness ("vanity")—of the things of life: work, wealth, pleasures, wisdom, death, and so on.

Key Verse
"Now all has been heard; Here is the conclusion of the matter: Fear God and keep his commandments, for this is the duty of all mankind" (Eccl. 12:13).

Song of Songs

Time/Place
Though Solomon is identified as the author in the first verse, some parts of the book appear to be written by others and were composed at a later date.

The Book
This book is a love song that moves from courtship, the wedding ceremony, and through the banquet celebration. Solomon himself had hundreds of wives (hardly an example of marital faithfulness!). Rather than a description from Solomon's own life, the song can be seen as an expression of an ideal experience within a loving, covenant relationship.

Key Verse
"I am my beloved's and my beloved is mine" (Song 6:3).

PARALLEL STORY LINES

The books of Samuel, Kings, and Chronicles cover about 500 years of Israel's history, from the end of the era of the judges to the fall of Judah in 586 BC.

The first book of Samuel tells what happened before David became king, focusing on the stories of the prophet Samuel, the first king Saul, and the young warrior David. The second book of Samuel along with both books of Kings cover roughly the same time period as the two books of Chronicles.

This gives us parallel accounts of the reign of the kings from King David to the eventual fall of Israel and Judah.

1 and 2 Samuel

Time/Place
The books of Samuel cover from the latter part of the era of the judges through David's reign and take place primarily in Judah. Some sections of the books may have been written by Samuel, Nathan, and Gad (see 1 Chron. 29:29–30).

The Books
These books illustrate God's blessing upon the faithful, the disastrous consequences of sin, and God's mercy when David repents.

Key Verse
"The LORD does not look at the things people look at. People look at the outward appearance, but the LORD looks at the heart'" (1 Sam. 16:7).

1 and 2 Kings

Time/Place
The books of Kings cover the time period from King Solomon's reign through the division and slow collapse of Israel and Judah.

The author is unknown, but Jewish tradition attributes the books to the prophet Jeremiah.

The Books
These books explain how the kingdoms of Israel and Judah were conquered and their people exiled because of their sins.

The books also include the stories of the prophets Elijah and Elisha.

Key Verse
"So give your servant a discerning heart to govern your people and to distinguish between right and wrong. For who is able to govern this great people of yours?" (1 Kings 3:9).

1 and 2 Chronicles

Time/Place
Both books of Chronicles were written after the exile, around 450–400 BC, by an unknown author. Jewish tradition attributes the book to Ezra.

The books cover a long period of history, from the death of King Saul to the fall of Judah and the exile.

The Books
These books were written to encourage the exiles who returned to Judah by connecting them to their history. The first nine chapters include detailed genealogies from Adam to Saul.

Key Verse
"If my people, who are called by my name, will humble themselves and pray and seek my face and turn from their wicked ways, then I will hear from heaven, and I will forgive their sin and will heal their land" (2 Chron. 7:14).

Prophecy in Psalms

When Jesus said that all of Scripture spoke of him, he specifically mentioned the Psalms: "Everything must be fulfilled that is written about me in the Law of Moses, the Prophets and the Psalms" (Luke 24:44). Psalms 2, 16, 22, 69, and 110 are the most quoted psalms in the New Testament. All of them anticipate and explain the identity of the promised Messiah. Psalm 110:1 is the most-quoted verse in the New Testament.

Prophecy in Psalms	Fulfilment in Jesus
"Why do the nations conspire and the peoples plot in vain? . . . Rulers band together against the LORD and his anointed" (Ps. 2:1–2).	Rulers conspired together to crucify Jesus (Acts 4:25–28).
"You will not abandon me to the realm of the dead" (Ps. 16:10).	God raised Jesus from the dead (Acts 2:24–34).
"My God, my God, why have you forsaken me?" (Ps. 22:1).	Jesus said these same words while on the cross (Mark 15:34).
"My mouth is dried up like a potsherd" (Ps. 22:15).	Jesus thirsted during his crucifixion (John 19:28).
"They divide my clothes among them and cast lots for my garment" (Ps. 22:18).	While Jesus was on the cross, the soldiers divided his garments (John 19:23–24).
"Into your hands I commit my spirit" (Ps. 31:5).	These were some Jesus' last words on the cross (Luke 23:46).
"Zeal for your house consumes me" (Ps. 69:9).	Jesus drove merchants out the temple for corrupting God's house (John 2:14–17).
"They put gall in my food and gave me vinegar for my thirst" (Ps. 69:21).	Soldiers at Jesus' crucifixion offered him wine vinegar mixed with gall (Matt. 27:34; John 19:29).
"Sit at my right hand until I make your enemies a footstool" (Ps. 110:1).	God made Jesus Lord of all (Matt. 22:41–46; Acts 2:34–36; 7:56).
"You are a priest forever, in the order of Melchizedek" (Ps. 110:4).	Jesus is our High Priest for eternity (Heb. 5:1-6; 7:15–17).
"The stone the builders rejected has become the cornerstone" (Ps. 118:22).	Jesus is the chief cornerstone rejected by unbelievers (Eph. 2:20; 1 Peter 2:6–7).

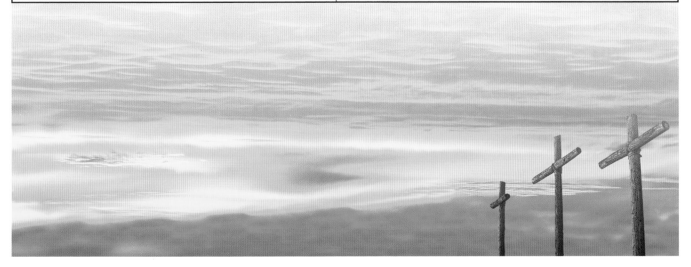

God gives Hannah a son, Samuel.
1 Sam. 1

The child Samuel hears God calling him.
1 Sam. 3

The ark is temporarily captured by the Philistines. Eli the high priest dies.
1 Sam. 4–6

Samuel leads Israel as a judge and prophet.
1 Sam. 7

1100 BC

Hannah's prayer of praise and Mary's song of praise (the Magnificat) are both in response to being blessed with a child from God. 1 Sam. 2:1–11; Luke 1:46–56

Both Samuel and David are listed as heroes of faith.
Heb. 11:32

David marries Saul's daughter Michal, befriends Saul's son Jonathan, and enters the king's army.
1 Sam. 18

After Saul tries to kill him, David spends 14 years as a fugitive.
1 Sam. 19–30; Ps. 18, 56, 57, 59, 63, 142

Samuel dies.
1 Sam. 25:1

David marries Abigail.
1 Sam. 25

TIME LINE KEY

 Prophecy Fulfilled by Jesus

 Person in the Genealogy of Jesus

 New Testament Connection

Dates are approximate.

Israel demands
a king. Samuel
anoints Saul.
1 Sam. 8–10

1051 BC

1050 BC

Saul disobeys God,
and God rejects
him as king.
1 Sam. 13, 15

Samuel anoints a
young shepherd
named David.
1 Sam. 16

David kills the
Philistine warrior
Goliath.
1 Sam. 17

David is listed in
Jesus' genealogy.
Matt. 1:6; Luke 3:31

David was
from the town of
Bethlehem and Jesus
was born in Bethlehem.
1 Sam. 16:1; Matt. 2:1

Saul consults a
medium at Endor
to speak to
Samuel's spirit.
1 Sam. 28

Saul and Jonathan
die in battle against
the Philistines.
1 Sam. 31; 1 Chron. 10

1011 BC

David is made king
of Judah in Hebron.
He rules from there
7½ years.
2 Sam. 2

David is made
king of Israel, then
conquers Jerusalem.
2 Sam. 5; 1 Chron. 11

In the New Testament, the designation
"Son of David" refers to the Messiah, one
who would establish an everlasting kingdom.
When blind Bartimaeus called Jesus "Son of
David," he could clearly see that Jesus was the
long-awaited Messiah. Mark 10:47

David writes many of the psalms in the book of Psalms.

David brings the ark to Jerusalem.
2 Sam. 6; 1 Chron. 13–16

Davidic Covenant: God makes a covenant with David.
2 Sam. 7; 1 Chron. 17

David sleeps with Bathsheba and has her husband Uriah killed.
2 Sam. 11

1000 BC

Psalms 2, 16, 22, 69, and 110 are the most quoted psalms in the New Testament. All of them point to the Messiah.

The angel Gabriel told Mary that she would have a son and God would give him "the throne of his father David, and he will reign over Jacob's descendants forever; his kingdom will never end."
Luke 1:32–33

Bathsheba is listed in Jesus' genealogy as "Uriah's wife." Matt. 1:6

Nathan and Bathsheba urge David to make Solomon (Bathsheba's son) king.
1 Kings 1; 1 Chron. 28

David dies after reigning 40 years.
1 Kings 2; 1 Chron. 29

971 BC

Solomon is made king, and God gives him wisdom and wealth.
1 Kings 3; 2 Chron. 1

Solomon builds the temple in Jerusalem on the threshing floor of Araunah.
1 Kings 5–8; 2 Chron. 2–7; Ps. 30

960 BC

Solomon is listed in Jesus' genealogy. Matt. 1:6–7

Jesus said, "Consider how the wild flowers grow. They do not labor or spin. Yet I tell you, not even Solomon in all his splendor was dressed like one of these. If that is how God clothes the grass of the field . . . how much more will he clothe you." Luke 12:27–28

Nathan rebukes David, and David repents.
2 Sam. 12; Ps. 51

Amnon assaults his sister Tamar.
2 Sam. 13

Absalom attempts a coup but is killed in battle.
2 Sam. 15–18; Ps. 3

A plague ceases when David buys the threshing floor of Araunah and builds an altar there.
2 Sam. 24; 1 Chron. 21

The queen of Sheba visits Solomon, admiring his wisdom and wealth.
1 Kings 10; 2 Chron. 9

Solomon writes parts of Proverbs, Ecclesiastes, and Song of Songs.

Solomon foolishly marries many foreign wives and worships their gods.
1 Kings 11

Solomon dies after reigning 40 years.
1 Kings 11; 2 Chron. 9

931 BC

950 BC

Jesus rebuked disbelievers for not recognizing that "something greater than Solomon is here," for even the queen of Sheba had recognized that Solomon's greatness was from God. Matt. 12:42

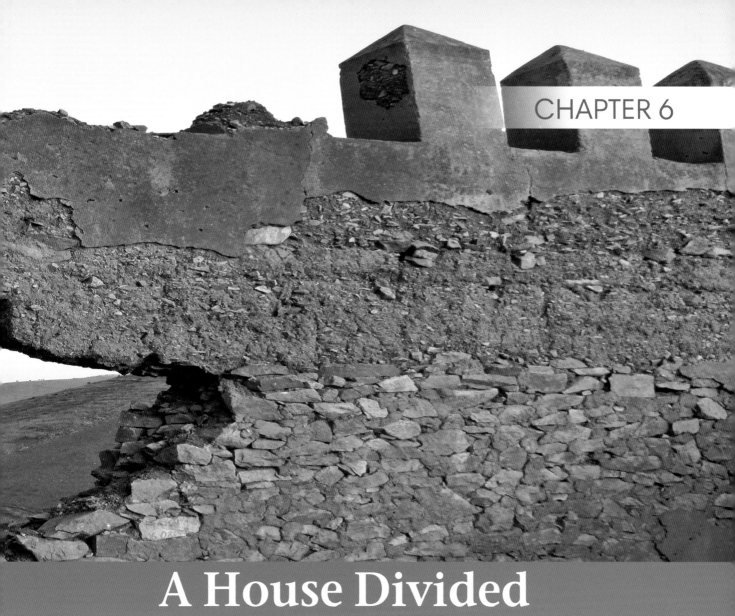

CHAPTER 6

A House Divided

From the Division of Israel to the Fall of Judah
950–600 BC

Elijah, Elisha, and the Kings

The Story of Jonah

Books of Isaiah, Jeremiah, and Other Prophets

After King Solomon's death, old tribal loyalties rumbling below the surface appeared again. Civil war broke out between the ten northern tribes and the two southern tribes. David had unified the tribes of Israel into a single kingdom, but now it was split in two. Eventually, both divisions of the kingdom would be conquered by outside invaders. As the words of Jesus remind us, a "house divided against itself will not stand" (Matt. 12:25 NKJV).

Kings and Prophets

1 Kings 12–22; 2 Kings 1–25; 2 Chronicles 10–36

In the south, King Solomon's son, Rehoboam, claimed kingship over the region of Judah. This territory became known as the Southern Kingdom of Judah. Under Rehoboam's rule, "the people engaged in all the detestable practices of the nations the LORD had driven out before the Israelites" (1 Kings 14:24).

In the north, Jeroboam, a former official in Solomon's court, was made ruler of the Northern Kingdom of Israel. With God's temple and the ark of the covenant in Jerusalem in the south, Jeroboam decided to give his people in the north new places of worship and new gods. Reminiscent of Aaron setting up the golden calf idol while Moses was on Mount Sinai (Ex. 32:4), Jeroboam set up two golden calves at the two ends of the Northern Kingdom and declared, "Here are your gods, Israel, who brought you up out of Egypt" (1 Kings 12:28).

These two wicked kings, Rehoboam and Jeroboam, were the first of a series of rulers—nineteen in Israel and twenty in Judah—most of whom did evil in the eyes of the Lord. God sent prophets to his rebellious people with words of warning. We read in the book of Amos about the prophet's warnings to an apathetic people who had turned their backs on God and exploited the poor and vulnerable. Despite military threats from powerful kingdoms like Assyria and Egypt, this was still a time of economic prosperity for Israel. And who would listen to prophets preaching doom when everything seemed to be okay? To keep Assyria and Egypt at bay, the kings of both Israel and Judah formed political alliances with these nations and adopted their gods and worship practices. The prophet Isaiah spoke out strongly against these alliances, but as was often the case, the kings didn't heed the prophet's warnings.

Notable for their wickedness were King Ahab of Israel and his wife Queen Jezebel. Since Jezebel was a Phoenician princess this marriage was likely a political union as well. Jezebel brought with her the worship of false gods, such as Baal, and she killed the prophets of God. Her husband King Ahab "did more to arouse the anger of the LORD, the God of Israel, than did all the kings of Israel before him" (1 Kings 16:33). When the prophet Elijah defeated the priests of Baal on Mount Carmel, Jezebel vowed to kill him. God intervened and

   Elijah in the Desert by Washington Allston, 1818

provided for Elijah, and in the end, God took Elijah up into heaven with a whirlwind (2 Kings 2:11–12). Jezebel and Ahab, however, both met violent deaths of their own (1 Kings 22:29–38; 2 Kings 9:30–37).

Despite the wickedness in the land, there were moments of spiritual revival. King Hezekiah of Judah "did what was right in the eyes of the LORD" (2 Chron. 29:2). Hezekiah's reign was almost 250 years after King Solomon had built the temple. By Hezekiah's time, God's people had abandoned the temple and abandoned him as their God. Hezekiah "opened the doors of the temple" and reinstituted worship, sacrifices, and the Passover (2 Chron. 29:3). Revival broke out and the people smashed their idols and tore down the altars to other gods.

Unfortunately, the kings who came after Hezekiah led the people astray again. God, in his patience, gave them yet another chance. About a generation after Hezekiah, Josiah came to the throne when he was only eight years old. The temple again had fallen into disrepair. Eighteen years into Josiah's reign, a discovery was made: the book of the law of God hidden away in the temple (2 Kings 22:8). When Josiah heard the Word of God read, he realized how unfaithful Judah had been to the covenant. Josiah destroyed the altars to foreign gods, celebrated the Passover, and read God's Word aloud so the people could hear it for themselves. In the presence of everyone, Josiah dedicated himself "to follow the LORD and keep his

commandments, statutes and decrees with all his heart and all his soul" (2 Chron. 34:31). But after Josiah's death, the four kings who came after him all did evil.

The Kingdom of Israel fell to Assyria in 722 BC and the Kingdom of Judah fell to Babylon in 586 BC. Second Chronicles 36:15–16 explains why the kingdoms fell: "The LORD, the God of their ancestors, sent word to them through his messengers again and again, because he had pity on his people and on his dwelling place. But they mocked God's messengers, despised his words and scoffed at his prophets until the wrath of the LORD was aroused against his people and there was no remedy." (See also 2 Kings 17:13–18.)

The prophet Jeremiah lived to see the fall of Judah. God delivered a message through Jeremiah for those who had been taken into exile, who had suffered under the cruelty of Assyria and Babylon—and this message was one of hope:

> When seventy years are completed for Babylon, I will come to you and fulfill my good promise to bring you back to this place. For I know the plans I have for you . . . plans to prosper you and not to harm you, plans to give you hope and a future. Then you will call on me and come and pray to me, and I will listen to you. . . . I will gather you from all the nations and places where I have banished you . . . and will bring you back to the place from which I carried you into exile. (Jer. 29:10–14).

Mosaic of the Prophet Jeremiah in the facade of Basilica of Saint Paul outside the walls. Rome, Italy. Millionstock/Shutterstock.com

Elijah and Elisha

God's Activity	Prophet's Activity	Event	Scripture
God Provides	Relies on God	During a severe famine, God sends Elijah food brought by ravens in the wilderness.	1 Kings 17:1–6
God Provides	Relies on God	Elijah stays with a widow and her son in Zarephath, and God miraculously provides them with a continual supply of flour and oil for food.	1 Kings 17:7–16
God Resurrects	Cries Out to God	When the widow's son dies, God raises the child from the dead, answering Elijah's prayer.	1 Kings 17:17–24
God Answers	Challenges False Prophets	Elijah calls down fire from the heaven and defeats the prophets of Baal on Mount Carmel.	1 Kings 18:1–46
God Encourages	Talks with God	Having fled into the wilderness when Queen Jezebel vowed to kill him, Elijah hears the voice of God in a gentle whisper.	1 Kings 19:1–18
God Instructs	Obeys God	Elijah obeys God and anoints Elisha to succeed him as prophet.	1 Kings 19:19–21
God Judges	Proclaims God's Judgment	Elijah tells King Ahab that the king and Jezebel will be judged for killing an innocent man, Naboth, and taking his vineyard.	1 Kings 21:1–29
God Judges	Proclaims God's Judgment	Elijah tells King Jehoram in a letter that the king will get an incurable illness because of his wickedness.	2 Chron. 21:12–15
God Judges	Proclaims God's Judgment	Elijah prophesies that King Ahaziah will die for consulting a foreign god.	2 Kings 1:1–18
God Takes	Received into Heaven	God takes Elijah to heaven in a whirlwind at the Jordan River as Elisha looks on.	2 Kings 2:1–12
God Speaks	Seeks a Divine Message	Elisha delivers a message from God about the battle Israel and Judah will fight against Moab.	2 Kings 3:11–19
God Intervenes	Works Miracles	Through Elisha, God does miracles in people's lives which confirm that Elisha's ministry is from God.	2 Kings 4:1–44; 6:1–6
God Answers	Prays	God answers Elisha's prayer for his servant's eyes be opened to see spiritual realities and the enemy blinded.	2 Kings 6:8–23
God Reveals	Prophesies Future Events	Elisha delivers messages about future events that all come to pass; the last is fulfilled after Elisha's death.	2 Kings 6:32–8:15; 13:14–25

Key Places of the Divided Kingdom

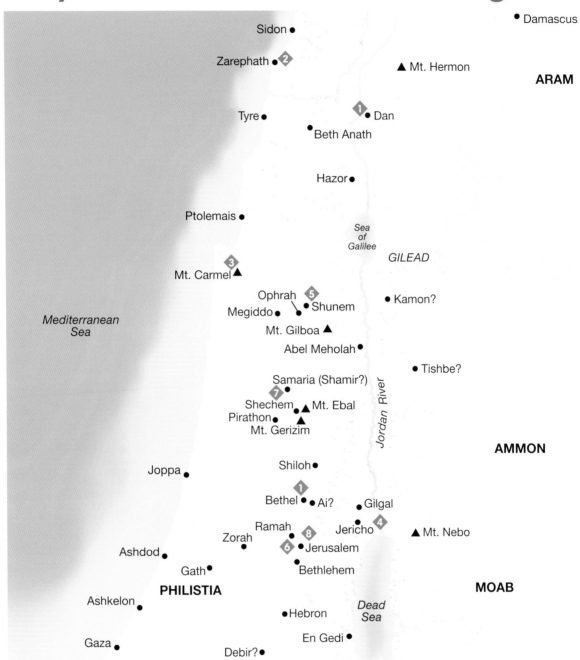

1. King Jeroboam sets up golden calf idols in Dan and Bethel. 1 Kings 12:26–30

2. Elijah raises a widow's son from the dead in Zarephath. 1 Kings 17:17–24

3. Elijah defeats the prophets of Baal on Mount Carmel. 1 Kings 18:16–40

4. Elijah is taken to heaven in a whirlwind at the Jordan River. 2 Kings 2:5–12

5. Elisha raises a woman's son from the dead in Shunem. 2 Kings 4:17–30

6. King Hezekiah restores the temple in Jerusalem. 2 Chron. 29:3–36

7. Samaria, the capital of the Northern Kingdom, falls to Assyria. 2 Kings 17:5–6

8. Jerusalem, the capital of the Southern Kingdom, falls to Babylon. 2 Kings 25:8–21; 2 Chron. 36:15–20

The Story of Jonah

We first meet Jonah in 2 Kings 14:25 during the reign of King Jeroboam II. There, Jonah prophesies that the king would restore the boundaries of Israel. But in the book of Jonah, the prophet's task is quite different from prophesying new victories for Israel. Instead, God called Jonah to deliver a message to Nineveh, the capital of Assyria: "Go to the great city of Nineveh and preach against it" (Jonah 1:2). At first glance, this would appear to be good news: God's judgment was about to fall on Israel's hated enemies. Israel, like all small kingdoms of the area, held no love for the Assyrians, who had a reputation for cruelty.

Surprisingly, however, "the prophet ran away from the LORD" (Jonah 1:3). Jonah boarded a ship on its way to deep sea. God sent a terrible storm that ended up with Jonah being thrown overboard by the crew. "The LORD provided a huge fish to swallow Jonah" and save him from drowning (Jonah 1:17). Jonah spent three days and three nights in the belly of the fish! There, he prayed to God.

After God commanded the fish to release Jonah, the prophet obeyed God and went to Nineveh. Surprisingly, the people of Nineveh, including their king, believed Jonah's message from God and repented. They fasted and covered themselves in sackcloth, a sign of contrition. "When God saw what they did and how they turned from their evil ways, he relented and did not bring on them the destruction he had threatened" (Jonah 3:10). But Jonah was not at all happy about this ending.

The last chapter in the book of Jonah is a dialogue between Jonah and God. The prophet complained, "I knew that you are a gracious and compassionate God, slow to anger and abounding in love, a God who relents from sending calamity" (Jonah 4:2). Think about that: Jonah had fled because he knew God was compassionate. God's intention to bless all nations was first seen in his promise to Abraham: "All peoples on earth will be blessed through you" (Gen. 12:3). God revealed something similar to the prophet Isaiah: "Blessed be Egypt my people, Assyria my handiwork, and Israel my inheritance" (Isa. 19:25). Jonah was angry that God's mercy and blessings was shared with Israel's enemy.

The story of Jonah ends with a question from God to Jonah: "Should I not have concern for the great city of Nineveh, in which there are more than a hundred and twenty thousand people who cannot tell their right hand from their left—and also many animals?" (Jonah 4:11). We don't know how Jonah responded to this question, if at all. The story leaves things opened-ended, letting readers reflect on how they would answer the question if they were in Jonah's situation.

Jonah

Time/Place
Jonah lived during the reign of Jeroboam II of Israel which was 793–746 BC, so the story in the book of Jonah is believed to have taken place around that time, but an exact date is uncertain. God sent Jonah to Nineveh, the capital of Assyria, Israel's enemy.

The Book
Somewhat different than other books of prophecy, Jonah is the most narrative (story-telling) in form. After spending three days and nights in the belly of great fish, the prophet obeyed God and went to Nineveh. When the Ninevites received God's mercy, Jonah became angry. Jonah's name means "dove."

Key Verse
"You are a gracious and compassionate God, slow to anger and abounding in love" (Jonah 4:2).

Amos

Time/Place
Amos prophesied to the Northern Kingdom of Israel, around 760–753 BC, some 30 years before it fell to Assyria.

Even though Amos was from a village near Bethlehem in Judah, he prophesied to the northern kingdom. His ministry centered in Bethel, the location of the king's temple in the north.

The Book
Amos was a shepherd and fig farmer called by God to prophesy against a materially prosperous Israel for treating the poor with injustice and betraying their covenant with God. Amos's name means "burden bearer."

Key Verse
"Hate evil, love good; maintain justice in the courts" (Amos 5:15).

Hosea

Time/Place
Hosea prophesied to the Northern Kingdom of Israel during a time of decline and eventual fall to Assyria, around 752–722 BC.

The Book
God instructed him to marry an unfaithful woman, Gomer, to serve as real-life illustration of Israel's unfaithfulness to their covenant with God and of God's unfailing love for his people. Hosea's name means "salvation."

Key Verse
"Go, marry a promiscuous woman and have children with her, for like an adulterous wife this land is guilty of unfaithfulness to the LORD" (Hos. 1:2).

Micah

Time/Place
Micah prophesied to Israel and Judah during the time of Israel's decline and fall to Assyria, around 738–698 BC.

The Book
Micah spoke against the leaders of Israel and Judah for their injustice, greed, and pride. But he also said that a remnant would return and regain their inheritance and worship the Lord. Micah's name means "who is like the Lord."

Key Verse
"He has shown you, O mortal, what is good. And what does the LORD require of you? To act justly, to love mercy and to walk humbly with your God" (Mic. 6:8).

MESSIANIC PROPHECIES IN ISAIAH

The book of Isaiah contains many prophecies that describe of a coming Messiah. The stories of Jesus Christ in the New Testament reveal how he fulfilled these prophecies.

Isaiah prophesied that:

The Messiah would be born of a virgin (Isa. 7:14; Matt. 1:20–23).

He would reign over the throne of King David (Isa. 9:6–7; Luke 1:31–33; 2:11), bringing freedom to the oppressed (Isa. 61:1–2; Luke 4:16–21).

He would be a descendant of Jesse, David's father (Isa. 11:1–2; Matt. 1:1–17).

He would also suffer as a servant (Isa. 53:1–12; 1 Peter 2:21–25) and proclaim the good news (Isa. 61:1–2; Luke 4:14–21).

Isaiah

Time/Place
Isaiah prophesied during the reign of four kings of Judah: Uzziah, Jotham, Ahaz and Hezekiah (Isa. 1:1). His ministry lasted more than 50 years, around 740–681 BC. He is also mentioned in 2 Kings 19–20, a story which parallels Isaiah 36–38. His name means "the Lord saves." He was married to a prophetess and had at least two sons (Isa. 7:3; 8:3)

The Book
Isaiah includes prophecies of judgment and salvation. Isaiah opposed Judah's alliances with pagan nations because God's people were relying on human power instead of God's promises. The prophet urged the people to repent of their sins and put their hope in the coming Messiah.

Key Verse
"For to us a child is born, to us a son is given, and the government will be on his shoulders. And he will be called Wonderful Counselor, Mighty God . . . " (Isa. 9:6).

Nahum

Time/Place
Nahum prophesied about a coming judgment upon Nineveh, the capital of Assyria, around 663–612 BC.

The Book
When Assyria defeated Israel in 722 BC, the people of Judah watched as the Assyrians tortured and deported the Israelites. Nahum's words were meant to warn the Assyrians to repent, but also to assure Judah that Assyria's sins would not go unanswered by God. Assyria fell to Babylon in 612 BC. Nahum's name means "the Lord comforts."

Key Verse
"The LORD is slow to anger but great in power; the LORD will not leave the guilty unpunished" (Nah. 1:3).

Zephaniah

Time/Place
Zephaniah prophesied to the people of Judah during the reign of King Josiah of Judah, around 641–628 BC.

The Book
The prophet warned about the judgment coming on the day of the Lord. It would be devastating to Judah and neighboring nations.

However, God promised that, in time, he would "gather the exiles," "bring you home" and "restore your fortunes before your very eyes" (Zeph. 3:19–20).

Key Verse
"The great day of the LORD is near—near and coming quickly. The cry on the day of the LORD is bitter." (Zeph. 1:1).

Jeremiah

Time/Place
Jeremiah prophesied to the people of Judah around the time of Judah's oppression and fall to Babylon (626–582 BC).

The Book
Sometimes called "the weeping prophet," Jeremiah pleaded with Judah to repent of their idolatry and arrogance. The people did not heed Jeremiah's message and he lived to see the fall of Judah to Babylon in 586 BC. The book of Jeremiah is the longest Old Testament book by word count.

Key Verse
"'For I know the plans I have for you,' declares the LORD, 'plans to prosper you and not to harm you, plans to give you hope and a future'" (Jer. 29:11).

Habakkuk

Time/Place
Habakkuk prophesied during a time of Babylonian oppression (609–598 BC), not long before Judah's demise at the hands of the Babylonians in 586 BC.

The Book
In this book, the prophet Habakkuk talks with God in a series of complaints and answers. He grapples with how God's anger and justice relate to God's love and mercy. Habakkuk's name might be derived from a Hebrew word meaning "embrace."

Key Verse
"How long, LORD, must I call for help, but you do not listen? . . . Why do you make me look at injustice? Why do you tolerate wrongdoing?" (Hab. 1:2–3).

Lamentations

Time/Place
The book of Lamentations dates to just after the fall of Judah to Babylon in 586 BC.

The Book
Lamentations is a series of five grief poems (laments) over the destruction of Jerusalem and the temple.

Although the book is anonymous, most traditions attribute it to Jeremiah. (Second Chronicles 35:25 indicates Jeremiah wrote several laments for King Josiah.)

Key Verse
"Though [the Lord] brings grief, he will show compassion, so great is his unfailing love" (Lam. 3:32).

Obadiah

Time/Place
Obadiah prophesied about Edom just after Judah fell to Babylon in 586 BC.

The Book
Obadiah is the shortest book in the Old Testament. The prophet pronounced judgment upon the people of Edom for their disregard and mistreatment of Judah. Although the Edomites were related to the Israelites (Gen. 25:30), Edom was an adversary of Israel in biblical history. Eventually, Edom also fell to Babylon (Jer. 27:3–6).

Key Verse
"Because of the violence against your brother Jacob . . . you will be destroyed forever" (Obad. 10).

Division of the kingdom:
After Solomon's death, his kingdom divides.
1 Kings 12–14; 2 Chron. 10–13
» Rehoboam: Southern Kingdom (Judah).
» Jeroboam: Northern Kingdom (Israel).

931 BC

Israel's King Ahab and Queen Jezebel kill the Lord's prophets.
1 Kings 16, 18

Elijah and Elisha prophesy to Israel.
1 Kings 17–21; 2 Kings 1–8, 13; 2 Chron. 21

Jonah spends three days and nights in the belly of a large fish.

900 BC   **800 BC**

Matthew traces Jesus' genealogy through Solomon's son Rehoboam, listing 13 of the kings of Judah. Matt. 1:7–11

Elijah and Moses appeared at the Transfiguration of Jesus. Matt. 17:3; Mark 9:4; Luke 9:30

James identifies Elijah's story as an example of how "the prayer of a righteous person is powerful and effective." James 5:16–18; see 1 Kings 17:1

Jesus said that, like Jonah in the fish, "the Son of Man will be three days and three nights in the heart of the earth." Matt. 12:39–40

King Hezekiah restores the temple; observes Passover.
2 Kings 18; 2 Chron. 29–32

716 BC

Hezekiah is healed of an illness; Isaiah prophesies to him.
2 Kings 19–20; Isa. 36–38

Nahum prophesies about Assyria's destruction.

Zephaniah prophesies about the coming day of the Lord.

King Josiah finds the book of the law and brings revival in Judah.
2 Kings 22–23; 2 Chron. 34–35

623 BC

700 BC   **650 BC**

Hezekiah is listed in Jesus' genealogy. Matt. 1:9

"The day of the Lord will come like a thief in the night."
1 Thess. 5:2

Josiah is listed in Jesus' genealogy.
Matt. 1:11

Amos prophesies to Israel.

Hosea prophesies to Israel.

Micah prophesies to Israel and Judah.

Isaiah prophesies to Judah.

Fall of Israel: Assyria conquers Israel. 2 Kings 17

722 BC

750 BC

Because of Jesus the Messiah, nations receive God's promises, as Amos prophesied. Amos 9:11–12; Acts 15:15–17

Jesus the Messiah was called out of Egypt, as Hosea prophesied. Hos. 11:1; Matt. 2:15

Jesus the Messiah came from Bethlehem, as Micah prophesied. Mic. 5:2; Matt. 2:4–6

Jesus declared that the prophecy of Isaiah 61 about the Messiah was fulfilled in him. Isa. 61:1–2; Luke 4:17–19

Jeremiah prophesies to Judah before and after its fall to Babylon.

The last four kings of Judah after Josiah all do evil. 2 Kings 23–24; 2 Chron. 36

Habakkuk prophesies in Judah.

Fall of Judah: Babylon conquers Judah; destroys the temple in Jerusalem. 2 Kings 25; 2 Chron. 36; Jer. 52

586 BC

Obadiah prophesies against Edom. Jeremiah writes Lamentations.

600 BC

Jeremiah spoke of "a new covenant" that God would make with his people. Jesus announced the arrival of this new covenant during the Last Supper saying, "This cup is the new covenant in my blood." Jer. 31:31; Luke 22:20

TIME LINE KEY

 Prophecy Fulfilled by Jesus

 Person in the Genealogy of Jesus

 New Testament Connection

Dates are approximate.

CHAPTER 7

A Time to Rebuild

From the Exile to the Return
600–400 BC

Daniel, Ezekiel, and Other Prophets

Ezra and Nehemiah

The Story of Esther

Where is God when everything is lost? That's the question the Israelites must have asked when they were exiled from their homeland. Their world as they had known it was shattered; their lives uprooted. For about twenty years, the powerful and ruthless Babylonian Empire invaded Judah, destroying homes, killing and starving the people, and taking the survivors off to distant lands.

During this era of biblical history, prophets like Ezekiel sent his people words of warning, but also words of hope for a coming day of restoration. The stories of Daniel and Esther reveal how God protected his people during life-threatening struggles in pagan lands. Leaders like Ezra and Nehemiah who returned to Jerusalem with other exiles faced the challenge of rebuilding a community both physically and spiritually in ruins.

Daniel

Daniel 1–12

Daniel was only a teenager when he was taken captive by the invading Babylonian army around 605 BC. He was deported from his homeland in Jerusalem and taken into service in the capital city of Babylon. Daniel, however, was determined not to live according to the standards of that world, but to God's standards. Much like Jesus' prayer for his disciples that they would be able to live *in* the world without being *of* the world (John 17:14–15), Daniel understood this well.

The stories in the book of Daniel paint a portrait of a man fully committed to living a holy life in the midst of a pagan land, unashamed of his God. His first test as a young man in training in Babylon was whether he would eat certain foods that violated God's law. He abstained from those foods, and God blessed him. When Daniel correctly interpreted King Nebuchadnezzar's dream of a statue, he gave God the glory instead of taking credit himself, much like Joseph when he interpreted Pharaoh's dream. Daniel told the king, "No wise man, enchanter, magician or diviner can explain to the king the mystery he has asked about, but there is a God in heaven who reveals mysteries" (Dan. 2:27–28). In Daniel's later years, he continued to pray publicly three times a day, even when the king prohibited it. This landed Daniel in a den of lions. But God was there with Daniel in the lions' den and he shut the mouths of the lions, saving Daniel from certain death (Dan. 6).

The book of Daniel also records a story about Daniel's friends: Shadrach, Meshach, and Abednego (Dan. 3). When they refused the king's command to bow down to an idol, the king threw them into a blazing furnace. God miraculously saved them through the fire, revealing to the king that God is the only one worthy of worship. For them, just like for Daniel, obedience to God trumped obedience to earthly kings. As Peter said to the rulers of his day in the New Testament, "We must obey God rather than human beings!" (Acts 5:29).

Daniel's Answer to the King
by Briton Riviére, 1892

Ezekiel

Ezekiel 1–48

While Daniel was navigating the royal court in Babylon, a priest named Ezekiel was living among the exiles in Nippur, a Jewish settlement by the Kebar River near Babylon.

Ezekiel was taken captive from Judah to Babylonia about eight years after Daniel was taken. We know much less about Ezekiel's life than Daniel's, only that Ezekiel was married and at some point his wife died (Ezek. 24:18).

Ezekiel was called by God to be a prophet, a "watchman" (Ezek. 3:17; 33:7). Think of a watchman in a high tower, vigilantly looking for approaching danger and warning the people when trouble is in sight. That was Ezekiel's prophetic mission—and it was not an easy one.

The book of Ezekiel consists of judgment prophecies, laments, and visions of Israel's future restoration. The first thirty-two chapters show the prophet delivering God's warning of coming suffering to Judah and other nations. Ezekiel tried to get the message across to the people in any way possible. He employed unusual imagery, even acting out the coming destruction of Jerusalem by shaving his head and baking bread over a fire fueled by cow dung (Ezek. 4:15; 5:1). Judah would experience a time of suffering because God was judging them for their idolatry, murders, sexual sins, exploitation of the vulnerable, and alliances with pagan nations (Ezek. 22:1–12). Ezekiel's message from God was surely a difficult one to deliver!

The remainder of the book (chapters 33–48) occurs after the fall of Jerusalem to the Babylonian Empire in 586 BC. In these chapters, Ezekiel offers a different message, one of hope out of the bleakness of suffering. God gave Ezekiel a vision of a valley of dry bones springing to life with new flesh, a reminder that death is never the final judgment for God's people.

> [Israel says,] "Our bones are dried up and our hope is gone; we are cut off." Therefore prophesy and say to them: "This is what the Sovereign Lord says: My people, I am going to open your graves and bring you up from them; I will bring you back to the land of Israel. . . . I will put my Spirit in you and you will live, and I will settle you in your own land."
> (Ezek. 37:11–14)

Ezekiel's last vision was in 571 BC, fifteen years after the fall of Jerusalem, but still decades before the exiles would return to their homeland (Ezek. 29:17). The prophet himself probably didn't live to see the end of the exile, yet he looked forward to a time when God would make all things right, where there would be a new glorious temple and a heavenly city whose name is literally "The Lord is there" (Ezek. 48:35).

Kingdoms in Daniel

The Statue Nebuchadnezzar's dream of an enormous statue (Dan. 2)	The Four Beasts Daniel's dream of four beasts from the sea (Dan. 7)	The Kingdoms Kingdoms symbolized by the statue and beasts
Head of Fine Gold Gold signified power and glory. In Daniel's time, Babylon was the most powerful and wealthy kingdom the ancient Near East had seen.	**Lion with Wings of an Eagle** Nebuchadnezzar is compared to both a lion (Jer. 4:7; 50:44) and an eagle (Ezek. 17:3–12). Images of winged lions were popular in Babylonian architecture and currency.	**Babylonian Empire** 605–539 BC King Nebuchadnezzar to King Belshazzar
Chest and Arms of Silver Media and Persia jointly were the second great power. They defeated Babylon.	**Bear with Ribs in Its Mouth** The bear being raised on one side may illustrate Persian dominance over Media. The three ribs may be the major empires Persia conquered.	**Medo-Persian Empire** 539–332 BC King Cyrus to King Darius III Persia is symbolized by a ram in Daniel 8.
Belly and Thighs of Bronze Bronze was of lesser value than gold or silver, symbolizing this kingdom's inferior status.	**Leopard with Four Wings and Four Heads** The wings may illustrate the speed of Alexander's conquest of Persia. The heads may be the division of Alexander's empire into four provinces after his death.	**Greece** 332–63 BC Alexander the Great and the four divisions Greece is symbolized by a goat in Daniel 8.
Legs of Iron; Feet of Iron and Clay This divided kingdom was as strong as iron, but was mixed with clay, a weaker substance. The Bible doesn't specifically identify this kingdom, but most scholars believe it to be the Roman Empire.	**Beast with Ten Horns** The horns are ten kings that would rise from this kingdom. Then another king ("little horn") would speak against God and persecute God's people. It's during this king's reign that God would set up an everlasting kingdom.	**Divided Kingdom** The Roman Empire: 63 BC through the time of Jesus
Rock Cut from a Mountain A rock, not crafted by human hands, struck the statue on its feet and broke it to pieces. The rock became a mountain that filled the whole earth. This symbolizes Jesus initiating the kingdom of God.	**The Son of Man** At the end of Daniel's vision of beasts, he saw "one like a son of man, coming with the clouds of heaven" who was given "authority, glory and sovereign power; all nations and peoples of every language worshiped him" (Dan. 7:13–14).	**Everlasting Kingdom** Jesus referred to himself as the Son of Man (Mark 10:45). The apostle John had a vision of Jesus Christ ("one like a son of man") ruling in heaven (Rev. 14:14).

Daniel

Time/Place
Daniel lived most of his life in Babylon, around 605–535 BC, during the reigns of kings Nebuchadnezzar and Belshazzar of Babylon and Cyrus of Persia (Dan. 1:1; 5:1; 10:1). Daniel's name means "God is my judge."

The Book
Chapters 1–6 recount stories of Daniel's and his friends' lives in exile. Chapters 7–12 contain Daniel's prophetic visions concerning the future.

Key Verse
"The God of heaven will set up a kingdom that will never be destroyed. . . . It will crush all those kingdoms and bring them to an end, but it will itself endure forever" (Dan. 2:44).

Ezekiel

Time/Place
Ezekiel ministered to the exiles in Nippur by the Kebar River near Babylon (Ezek. 1:1). His visions date from 593 BC (Ezek. 1:2) to 571 BC (Ezek. 29:17) during the reign of King Nebuchadnezzar of Babylon. Ezekiel's name means "God will strengthen."

The Book
Chapters 1–24 take place before the fall of Jerusalem in 586 BC and chapters 33–48 are after. The middle section, chapters 25–32, contains prophecies against foreign nations.

Key Verse
"I have made you a watchman for the people of Israel; so hear the word I speak and give them warning from me" (Ezek. 3:17).

Ezra

Time/Place
The book of Ezra tells the history of the exiles' return to Jerusalem in 538 BC, the rebuilding of the temple in 516 BC, and Ezra's reforms in Jerusalem about sixty years later.

The Book
Chapters 1–6 occur before Ezra's time, with Ezra's own story beginning in chapter 7 and continuing through the end of the book. Ezra, who was a priest and a scribe, is believed to be the author of both the books of Ezra and Nehemiah.

Key Verse
"'He is good; his love toward Israel endures forever.' And all the people gave a great shout of praise to the LORD, because the foundation of the house of the LORD was laid" (Ezra 3:11).

Nehemiah

Time/Place
Nehemiah's story takes place at first in Susa, the capital of Persia, and then in Jerusalem where the people rebuilt the city walls, around 444–432 BC.

The Book
The books of Ezra and Nehemiah were originally just one book. Nehemiah's story picks up where the book of Ezra left off.

Together, Ezra the priest and Nehemiah the governor brought social and spiritual reforms to Jerusalem.

Key Verse
"This day is holy to our Lord. Do not grieve, for the joy of the LORD is your strength" (Neh. 8:10).

Ezra and Nehemiah

Ezra 1–10; Nehemiah 1–13

The book of Ezra opens with the fulfillment of Jeremiah's prophecy: After seventy years of exile the Jews would return to their homeland (Jer. 25:11–12; 29:10; Ezra 1:1). In 539 BC, the great Babylonian Empire had fallen to Persia. God worked in the heart of King Cyrus of Persia, causing him to decree that the Jews could return to Jerusalem and rebuild their temple (2 Chron. 36:22–23). But by this time, many exiles had laid down new roots in these foreign lands and chose to stay where they were. Still, thousands of Jews were determined to make the trek hundreds of miles to go to Judah and start over yet again.

Under the leadership of Zerubbabel and Joshua the high priest, the people laid a new foundation to rebuild the temple in Jerusalem that the Babylonians had razed (Ezra 3:10). However, not everyone was happy with this new building project. Some of the people already living in the land bribed officials and threatened the builders, so much so that construction stopped. God sent the prophets Haggai and Zechariah to call the people to renew their resolve to complete the temple (Ezra 5:1). With the prophets' urging, rebuilding resumed, and in 516 BC, seventy years after its destruction, a new temple was built—the visible sign that God was with his people (Ezra 6:14).

The narrative in the book of Ezra then fast-forwards about six decades and introduces a priest and scholar named Ezra who "devoted himself to the study and observance of the Law of the LORD, and to teaching its decrees and laws" (Ezra 7:10). He led a large group of exiles on a four-month, nine-hundred-mile journey from Babylon to Jerusalem. Ezra instituted spiritual and social reforms to ensure that this new community in Jerusalem would obey God's law and avoid the sins that had led to the exile.

Meanwhile in the Persian capital of Susa, a Jewish man named Nehemiah served King Artaxerxes as his cupbearer (Neh. 1:11). Being a cupbearer to the king meant holding an influential position as a confidant of the king. When he heard that the walls of Jerusalem were in shambles, Nehemiah, whose name means "the LORD comforts," was thrown into distress. He persuaded the king to let him go to Jerusalem at once and lead the rebuilding effort.

Just like when the temple was being rebuilt, the construction of the city walls was met with opposition. The book of Nehemiah tells how Nehemiah and the people overcame this opposition and persisted in rebuilding their city. When the walls were complete, Ezra read God's law to the crowd and a renewed spirit of obedience to the Lord swept through the people. They observed the biblical festivals to remember God's faithfulness: "Nehemiah said, 'Go and enjoy choice food and sweet drinks, and send some to those who have nothing prepared. This day is holy to our Lord. Do not grieve, for the joy of the LORD is your strength'" (Neh. 8:10). As Ezekiel had seen in his vision of dry bones being brought back to life, the people of God, who had suffered immensely and must have felt like dry dead bones, were given new life and a reason to celebrate in the joy of the Lord again.

Journey of the Exile and Return

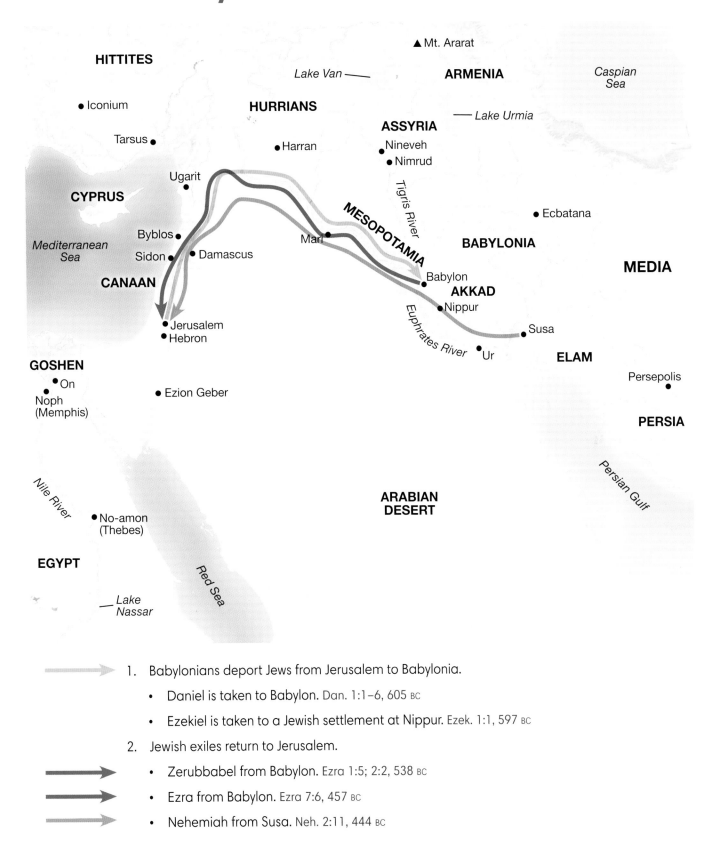

1. Babylonians deport Jews from Jerusalem to Babylonia.
   - Daniel is taken to Babylon. Dan. 1:1–6, 605 BC
   - Ezekiel is taken to a Jewish settlement at Nippur. Ezek. 1:1, 597 BC
2. Jewish exiles return to Jerusalem.
   - Zerubbabel from Babylon. Ezra 1:5; 2:2, 538 BC
   - Ezra from Babylon. Ezra 7:6, 457 BC
   - Nehemiah from Susa. Neh. 2:11, 444 BC

The Story of Esther

Esther's story took place in the Persian royal court in the capital city of Susa. The royal court was a place of power, where decisions, obsessions, and the whims of a handful of people decided the fate of thousands. The time period was in the fifth century BC during the reign of King Xerxes (Ahasuerus). In biblical history at this time, hundreds of miles away in Judah, exiled Jews had returned to Jerusalem and already rebuilt the temple of God. Yet many Jewish families had remained in foreign lands, having established new lives and homes. Esther's family was one that stayed in Persia.

Esther was a young Jewish woman, orphaned and raised by her older cousin Mordecai. In the story, King Xerxes was in search of a new queen and Esther was drafted into the contest to become royalty. Esther's Hebrew name was Hadassah, which means "star." On Mordecai's advice, this "star" hid her Jewish identity and blended into Persian society. (This was very different than what Daniel's approach had been in the royal court of Babylon.) Esther eventually won the king's favor and the orphan girl became the new queen of Persia.

A turning point in Esther's story came when she was faced with a life-threatening choice about her Jewish identity. A man named Haman convinced the king to issue an edict to kill all the Jews in the Persian provinces on a single day. It was to be a day of genocide! At first, Queen Esther was reluctant to intervene, but Mordecai convinced her: "And who knows but that you have come to your royal position for such a time as this?" (Est. 4:14). She chose the path of courage. She utilized her royal position and revealed to the king that she too was a Jew, one marked for his murderous edict.

By the end of the story, the tables had turned. The king ordered Haman's execution and gave Haman's estate to Mordecai. The king also permitted the Jews the right to defend themselves against anyone who tried to carry out the murderous edict against them, thereby saving them from annihilation. The festival of Purim (Feast of Lots) was established to commemorate this event (Est. 9:20–32).

The book of Esther is the only book of the Bible that does not explicitly mention God. This apparent absence, however, makes an important point: God's presence may not always be in the foreground—like the miraculous signs and wonders in the stories of Abraham and Moses—but his presences is behind the scenes. He works through the seeming coincidences of human events to bring about his will. The question that faced God's people in exile was this: Would God still protect them even though they were scattered in far off lands? The story of Esther answers this question with a resounding *yes!*

Esther

Time/Place
Esther's story is set in Susa, the capital of Persia, during the reign of King Xerxes (486–465 BC).

The Book:
Chapters 1–2 tell how Esther became queen of Persia. Chapters 3–5 explain how the lives of the Jews became threatened, and 6–10 how they were rescued and Purim (Feast of Lots) was established.

Key Verse
"And who knows but that you have come to your royal position for such a time as this?" (Est. 4:14).

Haggai

Time/Place
The book of Haggai dates to around 520 BC, more than a decade after the first group of Jews returned to Jerusalem under Zerubbabel. Haggai's name means "festival" and his ministry is mentioned in Ezra 5:1; 6:14.

The Book
God's message through Haggai was to call the people to evaluate how they were living. They were residing in nice houses while the house of God lay in ruins. Along with Zechariah, Haggai urged the people of Judah to continue rebuilding the temple.

Key Verse
"Is it a time for you yourselves to be living in your paneled houses, while this house remains a ruin? Give careful thought to your ways" (Hag. 1:4–5).

Zechariah

Time/Place
The book of Zechariah dates to around 520–518 BC. Zechariah's name means "the LORD remembers." He was a Jewish priest and was born in Babylon. He migrated to Jerusalem with the exiles who returned with Zerubbabel (Neh. 12:16).

The Book
Along with Haggai, Zechariah urged the people to continue rebuilding the temple (Ezra 5:1; 6:14). Chapters 1–8 contain visions and messages, and chapters 9–14 are oracles against sinful nations. The book of Zechariah reminds readers that God is sovereign and faithful to his promises.

Key Verse
"'Not by might nor by power, but by my Spirit,' says the LORD" (Zech. 4:6).

Malachi

Time/Place
Malachi prophesied in Judah, possibly during the time of Ezra and Nehemiah in the 400s BC. His name means "messenger," but little else is known about him.

The Book
Six prophetic speeches are recorded in the book of Malachi. These speeches call for spiritual renewal among a people who had largely given up on God.

Key Verse
"'Bring the whole tithe into the storehouse that there may be food in my house. Test me in this,' says the LORD Almighty, 'and see if I will not throw open the floodgates of heaven and pour out so much blessing'" (Mal. 3:10).

Joel

Time/Place
It's not known when Joel prophesied, but some scholars place his ministry either just before the exile in 586 BC or as late as the 400s–300s BC. Joel's name means "the LORD is God."

The Book
The focus of Joel's book is to call the people of Judah to repent before the coming of the great and dreadful day of the Lord.

Key Verse
"Blow the trumpet in Zion; sound the alarm on my holy hill. Let all who live in the land tremble, for the day of the LORD is coming. It is close at hand" (Joel 2:1).

Daniel is taken
to Babylon.
Dan. 1

605 BC

Daniel interprets King
Nebuchadnezzar's
dream of a statue.
Dan. 2

God protects
Shadrach, Meshach,
and Abednego in the
fiery furnace.
Dan. 3

Ezekiel is taken
into exile.

597 BC

600 BC

In Nebuchadnezzar's dream, a powerful rock
destroys the statue. This represents the establishment
of God's eternal kingdom—a kingdom that the angel
Gabriel told Mary her son Jesus would rule over forever.
Dan. 2:34–35; Luke 1:31–32

Ezekiel receives
news: Jerusalem
has fallen!
Ezek. 33

585 BC

Ezekiel prophesies
God's restoration
of Israel.
Ezek. 34–39

Ezekiel's vision
of a glorious
future temple.
Ezek. 40–48

Ezekiel's last
recorded
prophecy.
Ezek. 29:17–21

571 BC

Nebuchadnezzar
goes insane.
In the end, his
sanity returns
and he worships
God.
Dan. 4

TIME LINE KEY

 Prophecy Fulfilled by Jesus

 Person in the Genealogy of Jesus

 New Testament Connection

The 70 years of the exile
(see Jer. 25:11; 29:10) can be
measured from the destruction
of the temple in 586 BC to the
time it was rebuilt in 516 BC.

Dates are approximate.

Ezekiel receives
his calling to
be a prophet/
watchman.
Ezek. 1–3

593 BC

Ezekiel prophesies
God's judgment
upon Judah.
Ezek. 4–24

Ezekiel prophesies
God's judgment
upon the nations.
Ezek. 25–32

Fall of Judah:
Babylon conquers
Judah and destroys
the temple.
2 Kings 25; 2 Chron. 36

586 BC

The book of Ezekiel features imagery
similar to that found in John's visions in
Revelation: the throne room of God, the
eating of a scroll, an adulterous woman,
foreheads marked, and others symbols.

Daniel's vision
of four beasts
and a vision
of "one like a
son of man."
Dan. 7

Daniel's vision
of a ram and
goat.
Dan. 8

Daniel interprets
the writing on the
wall prophesying
King Belshazzar's
downfall.
Dan. 5

539 BC

Daniel's vision of an
"abomination" and
"seventy sevens."
Dan. 9

King Cyrus of
Persia allows
exiled Jews
to return to
Judah.
Ezra 1

538 BC

550 BC

When asked if he was the Messiah, Jesus
answered affirmatively and alluded to
Daniel's prophecy of a "son of man coming
with the clouds." In Revelation, John also sees
a son of man coming with the clouds. Dan. 7:13;
Mark 14:62; Rev. 1:7, 13

Jesus said Daniel's "abomination
that causes desolation" would be a
sign of the end times. Dan. 9:27; Matt. 24:15

First Return:
Zerubbabel and the high priest Joshua lead exiles to Jerusalem.
Ezra 2

538 BC

God protects Daniel in the lions' den.
Dan. 6

Daniel's last recorded prophecy: a vision of a man.
Dan. 10–12

535 BC

The temple foundation is laid, but it's not as glorious as the first temple.
Ezra 3

Temple construction stalls.
Ezra 4

Zerubbabel and Joshua are called "anointed" in Zechariah 4:14. *Christ* is the Greek word for the Hebrew word *Messiah* which means "anointed one."

Zerubbabel is listed in Jesus' genealogy. Matt. 1:13; Luke 3:27

In John's vision of the new Jerusalem in Revelation, there is no temple in the holy city because the Lord and the Lamb are its temple. Rev. 21:22

Ezra institutes social and spiritual reforms.
Ezra 9–10

Nehemiah hears that Jerusalem's walls are broken down.
Neh. 1

Third Return:
Nehemiah leads exiles to Jerusalem.
Neh. 2

444 BC

Under Nehemiah's governance, the walls of Jerusalem are rebuilt.
Neh. 3–7

450 BC

Haggai and Zechariah convince the people to resume rebuilding.
Ezra 5:1; 6:14

Temple construction is completed.
Ezra 6

516 BC

Queen Esther saves her people from annihilation.
Est. 1–8

Purim (Feast of Lots) is established.
Est. 9–10

Second Return: Ezra leads exiles to Jerusalem.
Ezra 7–8

457 BC

500 BC

✝ The book of Zechariah includes many messianic prophecies fulfilled in Jesus: the king coming to Jerusalem on a donkey; sold for thirty pieces of silver; people mourning for the one they pierced; and a shepherd struck and sheep scattered.

Ezra reads the law and the people confess their sins.
Neh. 8–12

Nehemiah goes to Persia for a short time, but then returns to Jerusalem.
Neh. 13

Malachi calls for spiritual renewal in Judah.

Joel prophesies about the coming day of the Lord.

400 BC

📖 Malachi prophesied that a special prophet would prepare the way for the Messiah. This was fulfilled in John the Baptist.
Mal. 3:1; 4:5 ; Matt. 11:10; Luke 7:26–28

📖 When the Holy Spirit came in power upon the disciples, Peter identified this event as the fulfilment of Joel's prophecy: "I will pour out my Spirit on all people." Joel 2:29; Acts 2:16–21

CHAPTER 8

A Changing World

Between the Old and New Testaments
400 BC–AD 1

Medo-Persia, Greece, and Rome

Herod's Dynasty

Pharisees and Sadducees

The Temple

For over one thousand years God had spoken to the Jewish people. From Moses to Malachi they had heard, repeatedly, the message of God's faithful covenant love for them coupled with his call for them to be faithful in return. Then, seeming silence descended as four hundred years passed between the prophet Malachi in the Old Testament and the angelic visits Luke describes in the first chapter of his gospel. But these years were anything but quiet on the world scene. Major shifts between powers and cultures took place during this time.

Though the history during this time period is not found in the sixty-six books of the Bible, what occurred here helps us see how God was using a changing world to prepare the stage for the entrance of the long-awaited Messiah.

Medo-Persia

Around 600 BC, King Nebuchadnezzar of Babylon had a dream of a huge, magnificent statue (Dan. 2). Only the prophet Daniel was able to interpret the what the statue meant. As Daniel explained, the four parts of the statue represented four successive kingdoms. These kingdoms are understood to be Babylon, Medo-Persia, Greece, and Rome.

By the close of the Old Testament in the 400s BC, the Babylonians had already fallen to the Medo-Persians. (The fall of Babylon occurred in 539 BC; see Dan. 5.) King Cyrus of Persia allowed the Jews to return to their homeland and rebuild their community. The temple in Jerusalem that had been destroyed by the Babylonians was rebuilt, along with the walls surrounding the city. Religious reform was also underway. The law of Moses was once again being stressed as central to Jewish life. Throughout most of this period, the high priests led the Jewish nation with very little intrusion by Persian kings.

One religious development during this time was the emergence of synagogues. These were local Jewish centers of worship and teaching. By the time of Jesus, synagogues were a very common sight. The New Testament writers tell how Jesus often taught in synagogues during his ministry (Matt. 4:23).

It was also during the Medo-Persian era that Aramaic became the dominant language among the Jews returning from exile. Aramaic was used in Babylon and it is related to the Hebrew language. In fact, Aramaic became so prevalent that eventually the Hebrew Scriptures had to be translated into Aramaic so that people could understand them when they were read. By the time of Jesus, Aramaic was still the everyday language spoken by Jews, making it the language Jesus spoke. Though the books of the New Testament were written in Greek, the gospel writers Matthew and Mark sometimes quote Jesus using Aramaic words (see for example, Matt. 5:22; 27:46; Mark 5:41; 7:34; 14:36).

Greece

In 336 BC, Alexander the Great began to conquer the Persian Empire at the age of twenty. Alexander's rapid and vast conquest of much of the Near East (subduing most of it in just three years) forever changed the culture of this entire area. This cultural shift is referred to as Hellenization, which was the spread of Greek culture, language, and religion.

As Hellenization occurred throughout the empire, Greek became the common trade language. This means that many people would have grown up knowing two or more languages. Even after the Roman Empire arose later, Greek was still the main trade language during the time of the New Testament. The New Testament books were written in Greek, making them easier to understand across the empire.

The untimely death of Alexander the Great at the age of thirty-two triggered a power struggle between his four generals. These generals fought to gain control over the vast empire that was left to them. After more than forty years of political struggles and warfare, four major divisions emerged: the Ptolemies, Seleucids, Antigonids, and Attalids. For over 150 years, the Ptolemaic and Seleucid dynasties held control over the Jews in Israel.

Ptolemy and his descendants (the Ptolemies) ruled Israel for over a century with a measure of respect for Jewish beliefs. The Jewish communities and their way of life and religion at this time were most threatened by the influence of Greek culture rather than war. Greek culture was polytheistic (belief in many gods), but the Jews were monotheistic (belief in one God). Their daily lives and behaviors reflected this stark difference. Adapting to Greek culture was seen by some Jews as undermining the uniqueness of Judaism and the God who had called them to be set apart. In response, many Jews focused daily life around synagogues in order to help preserve their one-of-a-kind faith and culture.

In 198 BC, Antiochus III defeated Ptolemy V, giving the Seleucids control over Israel. In contrast to a lot of the cultural and religious freedoms that the Ptolemies allowed the Jews, the Seleucids attempted to force the Greek culture and religion on them. Many Jewish practices were outlawed, such as circumcision, Jewish festivals, and even Sabbath observance.

In 188 BC, Antiochus III lost a four-year war against the Roman Republic when he tried to expand his territory. The Romans demanded that he and his descendants pay a massive tribute as terms for the peace agreement. The Seleucid rulers had to raise funds to pay the Romans. One such ruler was Antiochus IV Epiphanes. He accepted a bribe from Jason, the brother of a high priest, to not only be appointed as the new high priest in Jerusalem but also have the right to establish customs contrary to

Jewish law. This appointment outraged pious Jews. Antiochus IV saw the Jewish protest as an act of rebellion. As retribution, he stormed Jerusalem, ordered the murder of eighty thousand Jewish citizens, entered the temple, and took the sacred vessels. He desecrated the temple by sacrificing a pig on an altar to the Greek god Zeus and turned the temple into a temple of Zeus. The Jews were ordered to offer sacrifices to Greek gods, but many refused to the point of death.

In response, one man and his five sons took a stand against Antiochus IV and his decrees. In a small village northwest of Jerusalem, Mattathias, from the priestly family of the Hasmoneans, refused to make a sacrifice to Greek gods. When a fellow Jew took his place and attempted to make the sacrifice himself, Mattathias stepped in and killed both him and the Seleucid representatives. This marked the start of what became known as the Maccabean Revolt. The most notable of Mattathias's five sons was Judas, called Maccabeus or "the hammer." This family led a revolt of relentless guerilla warfare against the Seleucids and also against Jews who had compromised their religion. They would hide during the day and attack at night, destroying the altars that had been erected for Greek gods.

Their persistent and successful revolt eventually enabled Judas Maccabeus to lead an attack on Jerusalem, reclaiming the city and the temple from Seleucid control. The temple was cleansed and proper sacrifices were resumed with a dedication ceremony. This dedication became an annual festival that was celebrated through the time of Jesus (John 10:22) and is still celebrated by Jews today as Hanukkah.

When Judas Maccabeus died in battle in 160 BC, leadership was passed to his brothers in succession, establishing a line of Hasmonean rulers. Jonathan, Simon, and those who came later not only served as leaders in the struggle for Jewish independence, but also as high priests. This arrangement did not sit well with many Jews because the Hasmoneans were not descendants from the priestly line of Zadok. (See Ezek. 44:10–16 for prophecy about the Zadok priesthood.) It was around this time that the Pharisees and Sadducees began to emerge as distinct religious groups.

In 142 BC, Simon was finally able to break free from paying taxes to the Seleucids, bringing about freedom and self-rule for the Jews. However, discontent among the people about the leadership of the Hasmoneans only grew over time. The Pharisees in particular began to oppose the Hasmonean dynasty especially as the Hasmonean priests started to take on Hellenistic characteristics. Some Hasmoneans even ruled with harsh tyranny, like Alexander Jannaeus, who executed men, women, and children for opposing his rule.

Rome

The civil unrest during the Hasmonean dynasty weakened the Jews so much that Pompey, a Roman general, was able to gain control of Jerusalem fairly easily in 63 BC. The Jews would remain under Roman control through the time of Jesus and beyond.

An Idumean by the name of Antipater was appointed governor over Judea by Julius Caesar and given the task of uniting the area under Roman control. To accomplish this, Antipater's two sons, Herod and Phasael, were made rulers in the region. Herod was to rule over Galilee and Phasael over Judea as they sought to promote loyalty to Rome. However, in 40 BC the Parthians invaded the region, killed Phasael, and gained control of Jerusalem. Herod was able to escape back to Rome. In Rome, Herod was appointed king of Judea and was supplied with an army to take back control of Jerusalem. In 37 BC, Herod claimed victory, securing his rule in Jerusalem and the title Herod the Great.

During his reign, Herod was responsible for expansive architectural feats, including a harbor at Caesarea, several fortresses, and most notably, the expansion and renovation of the temple complex in Jerusalem. By the time of Jesus, this temple was viewed as one of the seven wonders of the ancient world. The temple in Jerusalem was the heart of Judaism because it represented God's dwelling among his people. Jews would travel to Jerusalem from all around to worship and make sacrifices, especially for the feasts of Passover, Pentecost, and Booths. But the temple also had a political significance. Herod the Great was half Jewish, but the Jews viewed him as a foreigner. Herod began the temple complex expansion as a way to curry favor with the Jews. The temple was connected with both the high priest and the Sanhedrin, the ruling Jewish judicial council. Social hierarchies were reflected in temple restrictions. While gentiles (non-Jews) could visit the temple, they were only allowed in the outer court and were forbidden to enter any other part of the temple complex, on pain of death. Women were allowed into the Court of the Women, but not the Court of the Israelites, which was closer to the temple center and reserved for Jewish men.

The Jews during this era responded to Roman rule and Herodian dominance in different ways. Two groups on opposite ends of the political spectrum were the Herodians and the Zealots. The Herodians were a Jewish political alliance of those who supported Herod and his sons who came to power after him. Many of the Herodians owed their elite status and wealth to Herod. This group is mentioned in the New Testament as siding with the Pharisees in their attempts to entrap Jesus (Matt. 22:16; Mark 3:6; 12:13). The Zealots, however, were defined by their *zeal* for Israel and the Jewish religion. They wanted to see Israel as its own kingdom once again, just like under King David. In Luke 6:15, one of Jesus' disciples is called Simon the Zealot, but scholars aren't sure if he was a political Zealot or only religious one—zealous for God's law, like the Pharisees.

Despite his many achievements, Herod was also known for being very paranoid—always afraid of losing his power. He not only had some of his own children executed, but also his wife, because he thought they were conspiring against him to take his throne. During Jesus' infancy, Herod notoriously ordered the death of male children aged two and under in or near Bethlehem in an attempt to kill the newly born "king of the Jews" (Matt. 2:1–18).

After the death of Herod in 4 BC, Emperor Augustus divided the rule of the region between Herod's surviving sons. Herod Antipas was established as tetrarch of Galilee and Perea. Much of Jesus' ministry took place in Galilee when Antipas ruled the region. Antipas was also the Herod who had John the Baptist beheaded and who questioned Jesus on trial (Matt. 14:1–12; Luke 23:7–12).

Pharisees and Sadducees

Probably the largest and most well-known Jewish religious group was the Pharisees. They began forming sometime after the exile and were probably fully established under the Hasmonean dynasty. Remember that the Jews had been both removed from their homeland and controlled by outside rulers. Their desire and need to protect their own identity, particularly as the chosen people of the one true God, became very important. The prophets in the Old Testament said that

the Jews' acceptance of corrupt beliefs and sinful practices were the reasons God had sent them into exile. To prevent another horrifying exile, the Pharisees' main goal was to make sure that Jews obeyed not only the Torah (law of Moses), but also the traditional interpretations of the Torah that had been passed down orally through the years. Doing or saying something contrary to this oral law was seen as the same as breaking God's law and also considered an act against the religious leaders. The Pharisees believed that purity rules, originally just for the priests, should trickle down to the home, so that every Jew lived a holy and pure life.

While the Pharisees may have been the larger and more popular group, the Sadducees held the most power. The Sadducees occupied priestly positions centered in the temple. They were not particularly popular with the average Jewish person because of their extreme wealth, influence, and political involvement. While

The Pharisees and the Herodians by James Tissot, between 1886 and 1894

the Sadducees' devotion to oral tradition and Scripture (other than the Torah) was weak, their punishments for infractions were severe, including death.

The Sadducees also dominated the Sanhedrin, the highest Jewish judicial council centered in Jerusalem. The high priest oversaw the Sanhedrin. Its members included elderly aristocratic nobles, chief priests, and Sadducees (who often were also aristocrats), as well as Pharisees and scribes. The Sanhedrin's decisions reached as far as capital punishment sentencing—though they could not enforce this apart from Roman cooperation. We see this play out in the New Testament accounts of Jesus' trial. After the Sanhedrin condemned Jesus, they handed him over to Pilate to make the final decision about Jesus' punishment (John 18:28–31).

JESUS AND THE PHARISEES

In the New Testament, the Pharisees appear to have had the most conflict with Jesus. Considering Jesus' association with known "sinners" and the "unclean," and that he taught as if he were an expert on God, such clashes with the Pharisees are not surprising.

In fact, we see the Pharisees joining forces with the Sadducees, their usual opposition, to confront Jesus and eventually bring about his crucifixion (Matt. 16:1).

Yet some Pharisees were receptive to Jesus' words (Luke 14:1) and some even became part of the Christian church (Acts 15:5). The Pharisee Nicodemus is one such example of a life changed by an encounter with Jesus (John 3:1–21; 7:50; 19:39).

Pharisees	Sadducees
From the Hebrew *paras*, suggesting "one who is separate."	Hebrew *seduqim*, "just/right ones"; originates from the name *Zadok* (Ezek. 44:10–16).
Established as a group during the Hasmonean dynasty.	Established as a group during the Hasmonean dynasty.
Laymen; with enough training they could become teachers of the law (rabbis) and scribes.	Priests and aristocrats; born into their positions of power.
Popular with the average person.	Favored by the elite.
Centered in synagogues.	Centered in the temple and the Sanhedrin, the Jewish ruling council.
Main Goal: To obey the Torah and the traditional interpretations of the Torah.	Main Goal: To keep Judaism centered on the sacrificial system at the temple.
Accepted all the Hebrew Scriptures including the Torah, as well as oral law.	Accepted only the Torah, the first five books of the Hebrew Scriptures.
Believed in resurrection, angels, and demons.	Did not believe in resurrection, angels, or demons (Matt. 22:23–33; Acts 23:8).
Refused to adapt to Greek/Roman culture, but also tried to avoid direct conflict with the ruling powers.	Allowed outside rulers and cultures to maintain power as long as the temple sacrifices continued.
Survived after the temple's destruction in AD 70 and developed as rabbinical authorities.	Disappeared from history after the temple's destruction in AD 70.

Hope for a Messiah

Life for the Jewish people under Roman rule can be characterized by extremes. On one hand, they were given freedom to work, live, and worship. But on the other hand, they were also constantly reminded that they were not truly free. Roman soldiers occupied their land continually. The burden of high taxes paid to Rome drove many people into poverty or slavery. Even their religious expressions were restricted in such a way so as to ensure that Rome was never challenged. Prophets who came proclaiming God's judgment were not tolerated—as seen in the arrest and execution of John the Baptist (Matt. 14:1–12).

The Jews longed for a day when they could truly be free, something that the prophets had promised with the coming of the Messiah. (The term *messiah* is Hebrew for "anointed one," called so because the king was set apart by being anointed with oil poured over his head.) As Isaiah had prophesied: "He will be called Wonderful Counselor, Mighty God, Everlasting Father, Prince of Peace. . . . He will reign on David's throne and over his kingdom, establishing and upholding it with justice and righteousness" (Isa. 9:6–7).

Most Jews held to the belief in a coming Messiah. However, they disagreed about what they thought this Messiah would do. In general, they believed that the Messiah would be a human who was aided in some way by God to do amazing, miraculous things—a king of Israel and descendant of King David. However, some, perhaps influenced by more secular thinking at the time, held that the Messiah was more of a concept that would enable the nation of Israel to come together and overthrow the rulers oppressing them.

Whatever their understanding, there was a general longing for a conquering king who would come and crush their oppressors and free them, establishing Israel as a prosperous nation once again. So when a miracle-working, humble young man from Nazareth burst onto the scene challenging the established religious authorities and loving even Roman authority figures, even his own disciples were confused. They had not envisioned a Messiah like him; one who would fulfill a promise from God given not only to David, but all the way back to Abraham—a king who rescues not only the Jews, but the whole world, from our greatest enemies: sin and death.

Herod's Dynasty

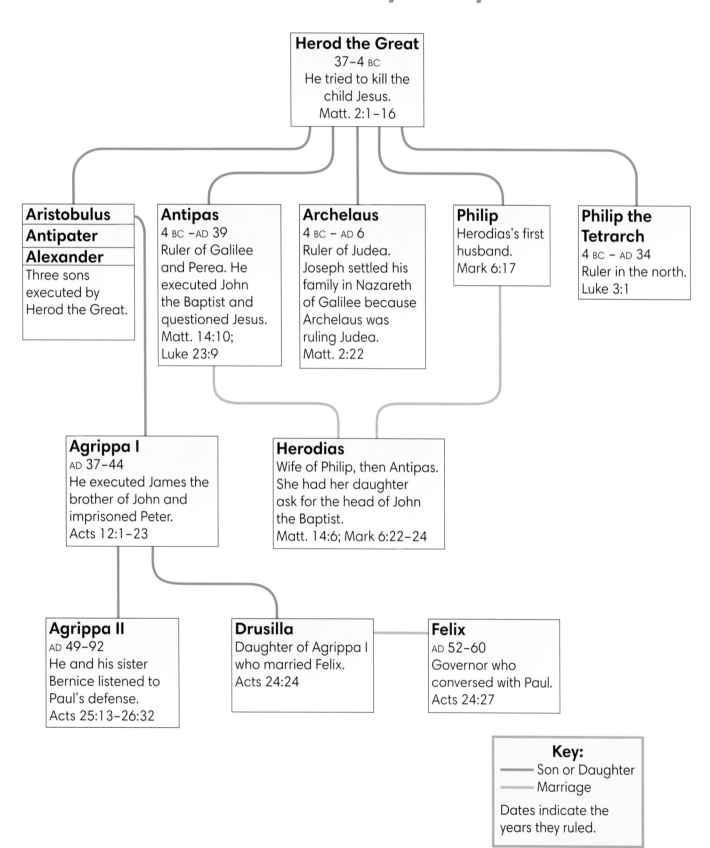

Herod the Great
37–4 BC
He tried to kill the child Jesus.
Matt. 2:1–16

Aristobulus
Antipater
Alexander
Three sons executed by Herod the Great.

Antipas
4 BC –AD 39
Ruler of Galilee and Perea. He executed John the Baptist and questioned Jesus.
Matt. 14:10;
Luke 23:9

Archelaus
4 BC – AD 6
Ruler of Judea. Joseph settled his family in Nazareth of Galilee because Archelaus was ruling Judea.
Matt. 2:22

Philip
Herodias's first husband.
Mark 6:17

Philip the Tetrarch
4 BC – AD 34
Ruler in the north.
Luke 3:1

Agrippa I
AD 37–44
He executed James the brother of John and imprisoned Peter.
Acts 12:1–23

Herodias
Wife of Philip, then Antipas. She had her daughter ask for the head of John the Baptist.
Matt. 14:6; Mark 6:22–24

Agrippa II
AD 49–92
He and his sister Bernice listened to Paul's defense.
Acts 25:13–26:32

Drusilla
Daughter of Agrippa I who married Felix.
Acts 24:24

Felix
AD 52–60
Governor who conversed with Paul.
Acts 24:27

Key:
—— Son or Daughter
—— Marriage
Dates indicate the years they ruled.

Chronology of the Temple

The temple (and earlier the tabernacle) was the place where God met with his people. It was a visible expression of God's desire to dwell among his people.

1. Tabernacle
Moses builds the tabernacle in the wilderness.
Ex. 25:8–9; 1446 BC

2. Promised Land
Joshua brings the tabernacle into the promised land and sets it up at Shiloh.
Josh. 18:1; 1406 BC

4. King Solomon
King Solomon builds the first temple in Jerusalem, replacing the tabernacle.
1 Kings 6:1; 960 BC

3. King David
David purchases a threshing floor, the site where the temple would later be built.
2 Sam. 24:21; 1000 BC

5. King Josiah
After years of the temple being corrupted, Josiah discovers the book of the law in the temple and then restores the temple.
2 Kings 22–23; 2 Chron. 34–35; 623 BC

6. Babylonian Destruction
The Babylonians conquer Jerusalem, and plunder and set fire to the temple.
2 Kings 25:8–9; 586 BC

7. Zerubbabel

Under Zerubbabel's governance, the Jews return from exile and rebuild the temple in Jerusalem, but it's not as glorious as the previous temple.

Ezra 3:12; 6:15; 516 BC

8. Rededication

Antiochus IV Epiphanes defiles the temple, but the Maccabean Revolt restores Jerusalem to Jewish control and the temple is rededicated (Hanukkah).

164 BC

10. Jesus at the Temple

During Jesus' ministry, he enters the temple courts and casts out merchants, heals the sick, teaches his followers, and prophesies that "not one stone here will be left on another."

Matt. 21:12–14; Mark 13:2; Luke 21:37;. AD 27–30

9. Herod the Great

Herod begins a massive expansion of the temple complex.

20 BC

11. Jesus on the Cross

At the moment of Jesus' death on the cross, the thick temple curtain is torn in two from top to bottom.

Matt. 27:51; see also Heb. 10:19–20; AD 30

12. Roman Destruction

To quell an uprising, the Romans massacre thousands in Jerusalem, pillage the temple treasures, and destroy the temple by setting it on fire.

AD 70

Aramaic becomes
the spoken language
among Jews.

Greece: Alexander
conquers Judea;
Hellenization begins.

332 BC

Alexander dies
and his kingdom
is divided.

323 BC

Greek becomes the
dominant language
across the empire.

400 BC

320 BC

300 BC

Ptolemy captures
Jerusalem by attacking
on the Sabbath.

Hasmonean
dynasty begins.

164 BC

Hasmoneans take
control of the
priesthood.

152 BC

Hasmonean Alexander
Jannaeus begins a
tyrannical rule.

Pharisees and
Sadducees become
established groups.

Hasmonean Simon
is made both king of
Judea and high priest.

100 BC

63 BC

Rome: Pompey
conquers Jerusalem
for Rome, ending the
Hasmonean dynasty.

Dates are approximate.

Seleucids begin to rule Judea.

198 BC

Antiochus IV Epiphanes desecrates the temple in Jerusalem.

167 BC

Hanukkah: Maccabean Revolt is successful and the temple is rededicated.

164 BC

200 BC

188 BC

Antiochus III is forced to pay a high tribute to the Roman Republic.

166 BC

Maccabean Revolt: Judas Maccabeus leads a Jewish uprising.

Herod the Great captures Jerusalem and rules Judea under Roman authority.

37 BC

Herod begins a massive expansion of the temple complex.

20 BC

Birth of Christ: Jesus born in Bethlehem. Luke 2:1–7

4 BC

27 BC

Caesar Augustus becomes the first Roman Emperor.

5 BC

John the Baptist is born. Luke 1:57–80

AD 1

Herod orders the death of all male babies in Bethlehem in an attempt to kill Jesus, the newly born "king of the Jews." Not long after, Herod dies. Matt. 2:1–19

CHAPTER 9

The Son of God

From Bethlehem to Jerusalem
AD 1–30

Life and Ministry of Jesus

Genealogy of Jesus

Harmony of the Gospels

The first four books of the New Testament—the gospels of Matthew, Mark, Luke, and John—tell the story of the life and ministry of Jesus Christ the Son of God. These books show in stunning detail how Jesus of Nazareth fulfilled Old Testament prophecies about the long-awaited Messiah—the anointed one sent by God to save his people.

Birth of Christ

Matthew 1–2; Luke 1–2

One would expect the arrival of the Messiah to have been a major, national event for the Jewish people, right?

It was anything but.

Of the four gospels, only Luke and Matthew say anything about the birth of Jesus. Both gospel writers describe angelic visits to Joseph and Mary—a kind of heavenly heads-up to a humble, unsuspecting couple. The angelic message was straightforward, yet astounding: Mary, a betrothed virgin, would give birth to the Messiah (*Christ* in Greek). He would be called Jesus—a variant of the name Joshua, which means "salvation"—because he would "save his people from their sins" (Matt. 1:21). He would also be called Son of the Most High and *Immanuel*, meaning "God with us" (Matt. 1:23). He would establish a kingdom that would never end (Luke 1:32–33).

On the night of Jesus' birth in the town of Bethlehem, the city of David, only a small band of stunned shepherds came to see the newborn baby—and this was only because they'd just heard about the event from an enthusiastic multitude of angels. Some days (possibly weeks) later, magi or "wise men" from the east showed up at the house where Jesus was. They worshiped him, showered him with gifts, and left. Had it not been for these two groups, it's doubtful that anyone but a handful of people would have been aware that the Messiah had just been born. In fact, it was only when the magi stopped first in Jerusalem asking questions about a "newborn king" that King Herod the Great became paranoid and concocted a murderous plot to eliminate all young boys in and around Bethlehem. Warned in a dream about Herod's intentions, Joseph and Mary fled to Egypt with Jesus. After Herod died, they settled in Nazareth of Galilee.

The gospels tell us very little about Jesus' childhood. What we do know from some statements made in the gospels is that Jesus had siblings and that he probably learned the business of carpentry from Joseph (Mark 6:3). There is, however, one intriguing story about a Passover visit to Jerusalem when Jesus was twelve years old. When his parents realized that they had started home without Jesus (after wrongly assuming he was traveling back home with other relatives), they backtracked and searched frantically for him. They located Jesus three days later at the temple in Jerusalem where he had astonished the teachers of the law with his spiritual insights. Luke explains that Jesus "grew and became strong; he was filled with wisdom, and the grace of God was on him" (Luke 2:40).

Early Ministry

Matthew 3–4; Mark 1; Luke 3–4; John 1–4

When Jesus was about the age of thirty, many people were streaming into the wilderness northeast of Jerusalem to listen to a fiery, mesmerizing prophet named John. (Jesus was actually a relative of John; see Luke 1:36.) John was calling people to repent and prepare for the Messiah's coming. John was baptizing in the Jordan River all those who were receptive to his message. When some people began asking if he was the promised Messiah, John quickly insisted that he was only a lowly servant preparing the way for God's anointed: "One who is more powerful than I will come, the straps of whose sandals I am not worthy to untie" (Luke 3:16).

Shortly after this, Jesus, the carpenter from Nazareth, stepped out of the crowd. John pointed at him and declared that he was "the Lamb of God, who takes away the sin of the world" (John

1:29). Jesus was baptized by John to identify with John and his message and the sinners Jesus had come to save. At Jesus' baptism, he was anointed by the Holy Spirit coming down from heaven in the form of a dove and affirmed as the Son of God by an audible voice from heaven. Then, immediately, he was led by the Holy Spirit into the wilderness to overcome the temptations of the devil (Mark 1:12–13).

After these events, Jesus began a three-year public ministry. He gathered a few disciples and quickly began to shock them with his words and works.

At a wedding in Cana of Galilee, Jesus miraculously changed water into wine, his first recorded miracle (John 2:1–11). Not only did this miracle reveal that Jesus was no mere man, but it also suggested that he had come to bring ultimate joy. Wine in the Bible is a symbol of gladness and blessing: "The Lord Almighty will prepare a feast of rich food for all peoples, a banquet of aged wine" (Isa. 25:6).

He Wept over It by Enrique Simonet, 1892

In Jerusalem for the feast of Passover, Jesus angrily drove merchants from the temple courts. He reflected God's disgust with empty religion, and he displayed a "zeal" for God's house just as the Scriptures said the Messiah would (Ps. 69:9; John 2:17).

While in Jerusalem, Jesus had a lengthy spiritual conversation with a Pharisee named Nicodemus, one of Israel's most prominent religious leaders. The gist of Jesus' message was that spiritual rebirth, not religious effort, is what makes a person right with God: "Very truly I tell you, no one can see the kingdom of God unless they are born again" (John 3:3).

In Samaria, Jesus stunned his disciples by demonstrating grace to a Samaritan woman at Jacob's Well. Through her testimony, many Samaritans came to believe in Jesus (John 4:1–42). Jews in Jesus' day usually avoided the region of Samaria and looked down upon the Samaritan people. Jesus' actions showed his love for all people.

Christ and Samaritan Woman by Henryk Siemiradzki, 1890

First-century Jewish rabbis typically selected their students from among the brightest and best, those actively pursuing advanced training in the Mosaic law. Not Jesus. At the beginning of his ministry, he plucked unlikely disciples out of fishing boats and tax offices. These were "unschooled, ordinary men" (Acts 4:13), not the sort around whom most leaders would try to build a religious movement. He spent the bulk of his time with these twelve men, inviting them to watch and learn from him. He wanted them to become disciples who would make disciples.

Teachings and Miracles

Matthew 5–20; Mark 2–10; Luke 5–19; John 5–12

Jesus taught constantly, sharing the deep truths of God. He taught in synagogues, the temple courts, people's homes, and outdoor settings. He preached in all sorts of contexts to huge crowds and small groups. He often seized on "chance" encounters to illustrate and explain spiritual truths to spiritually curious individuals. His authoritative words always left people scratching their heads in amazement: "When Jesus had finished saying these things, the crowds were amazed at his teaching, because he taught as one who had authority, and not as their teachers of the law" (Matt. 7:28–29).

He delivered a wide range of messages in which he touched on a host of topics: anger, resolving conflict, adultery, divorce, revenge, prayer, fasting, worry, religious persecution, the future, the Holy Spirit, servanthood, finding true rest, and so much more. Often in his discourses, he highlighted the sharp differences between God's kingdom and the kingdom of this world. In his famous Sermon on the Mount, he made clear the differences between these two ways of living (Matt. 5–7).

In the Kingdom of This World	In Christ's Kingdom
Only those who are competent and "together" are welcomed.	Only those who know they are desperate and needy are accepted (Matt. 5:3).
Suffering for any reason is to be avoided.	Suffering for righteousness is expected and will be rewarded (Matt. 5:10–12).
You treat others the way they treat you.	You show your enemies extravagant forgiveness and love (Matt. 5:38–48).
You do good things in order to be noticed and praised by others.	You do good things quietly, without any thought of impressing others (Matt. 6:1–6).
You stockpile all the wealth you can.	You store up treasures in heaven (Matt. 6:19–21).
You spend a lot of time and energy obsessing over clothing and food and such matters.	You concern yourself with spiritual and eternal matters (Matt. 6:33).
You point out and critique the flaws of others.	You focus on your own shortcomings (Matt. 7:1–5).
You're expected to go along with the crowd.	You're called to take the narrow road that leads to life (Matt. 7:14).

Jesus also taught in parables. In fact, of the recorded teachings of Jesus, about a third are parables. Parables are short, memorable, image-rich stories that reveal a truth about God or about how his kingdom works. They include stories like the one about the good Samaritan, which challenged listeners to consider what it really means to love your neighbor; and the parable of the prodigal son, which revealed God's unending love for all his children. To the spiritually disinterested, parables didn't mean much. To the spiritually hungry, however, parables packed a punch. Each one prompted healthy soul-searching, and called for a response to a certain heavenly reality.

As Jesus was preaching the gospel and teaching about the kingdom of God, he punctuated his ministry with breathtaking miracles. His ministry involved "healing every disease and sickness among the people" (Matt. 4:23). Jesus gave sight to the blind and hearing to the deaf. He corrected deformities and cured paralysis. Sometimes he healed by physically touching the sick, and sometimes the sick found healing by simply touching him. On some occasions, he made people whole by speaking a word from a distance.

These wondrous acts weren't tricks performed to impress others or to draw a crowd. On one level, they stemmed from the fathomless compassion of Jesus. When he saw hurting, needy people, he was moved to alleviate their suffering. On another level, these miracles functioned as "signs" (John 2:11). A sign often points to something else. The miracles of Jesus were designed to point people's attention to the person of Jesus. The miracles of Jesus authenticated his message. In other words, his miracles demonstrated the truth of his claims to be the God-sent Savior of the world.

Jesus' miracles also proved his absolute authority over the spiritual and physical world. "Many who were demon-possessed were brought to him, and he drove out the spirits with a word and healed all the sick'" (Matt. 8:16). He calmed stormy seas and even walked on them. He fed massive crowds with only meager amounts of food. On at least three occasions, Jesus resurrected dead people! Following each miraculous event, onlookers were left to marvel. When the disciples had watched Jesus command a stormy sea to become placid, "they were terrified and asked each other, 'Who is this? Even the wind and the waves obey him!'" (Mark 4:41).

Almost from the start of his public ministry, Jesus was immensely popular with the masses. Stories of him feeding thousands and performing other wonders went "viral" and resulted in enormous crowds. Yet the longer Jesus ministered, the more he infuriated the Jewish religious leaders. He shattered expectations and defied human traditions. From the beginning, Jesus made it clear that he had not come "to abolish the Law or the Prophets . . . but to fulfill them" (Matt. 5:17). He always displayed the utmost reverence for God's Word. However, he had zero patience for man-made religious rules. He riled the Pharisees, telling them, "You have a fine way of setting aside the commands of God in order to observe your own traditions!" (Mark 7:9). Not only did Jesus confront their hypocrisy and haughtiness at every turn, but

▶▶▶ HOW LONG WAS JESUS' MINISTRY?

One way to measure the length of Jesus' public ministry is by counting the number of Passovers in John's gospel. John is the writer most concerned with giving readers details about the Jewish festivals that happened during Jesus' ministry. John mentions four Passovers (John 2:13; 5:1; 6:4; 13:1); the first one very early in Jesus' ministry and the last one in Jesus' final week in Jerusalem. (Though John 5:1 doesn't use the word Passover, the festival mentioned is believed to be either Passover itself or another festival near the Passover season.) This means that Jesus' ministry continued for at least three years.

he also attacked the religious systems they had put in place to take advantage of others.

Jesus also raised eyebrows in the way he elevated women in a culture that viewed them as second-class citizens (John 4). People were scandalized by the way he honored little children and treated social outcasts with dignity (Matt. 8:3; 19:13–15; Mark 2:16).

Mostly, however, Jesus shattered the public's prevailing understanding of the Messiah. In the first century, the Jews were under Roman rule and messianic hopes were at a fever pitch. When would God restore the kingdom to Israel? Where was the deliverer who, in the spirit and manner of King David, would galvanize the people, lead a revolt, and drive the Roman pagans from the Jewish homeland? These were the questions on every heart and tongue.

Not long after Jesus began his ministry, many Jews had become convinced that Jesus would be this military deliverer. Yet when they tried to push Jesus in this direction, he resisted. He was clear about his mission. From the beginning, Jesus stated that he was sent *by* God to do the will *of* God: "For I have come down from heaven not to do my will but to do the will of him who sent me" (John 6:38). According to Jesus, God's will for him was to preach the good news of God's kingdom, call sinners to repentance, testify to the truth, bring light to a dark world, and drive out the devil. Jesus was the divine King and Messiah, but he was one who "did not come to be served, but to serve" (Mark 10:45). Bottom line, he came to save the world. And to do so, he would go to a cross on a hill in Jerusalem to lay down his life.

Matthew

Time/Place

This gospel was written by Matthew (Levi) a tax collector who became one of the twelve disciples (Matt. 9:9). It was written in the AD 60s or later.

The Book

As the most *prophetic* gospel, Matthew quotes extensively from the Old Testament and focuses on the teachings of Jesus the Messiah King.

This gospel covers the birth of Jesus and his public ministry through the resurrection appearances. Matthew concludes with the Great Commission (Matt. 28:19–20).

Key Verse

"Do not think that I have come to abolish the Law or the Prophets; I have not come to abolish them but to fulfill them" (Matt. 5:17).

Mark

Time/Place

This gospel was written by John Mark an early believer and helper to the apostles Paul and Peter (Acts 12:12; Col. 4:10). It's believed to have been the earliest of the four gospels, written possibly in the AD 50s.

The Book

As the most *practical* gospel, Mark focuses on the actions of Jesus the divine Servant. Mark highlights the humanity of Jesus, mentioning strong emotions like anger, compassion, and sorrow (Mark 3:5; 6:34; 14:33–34). It's a fast paced, action-oriented narrative starting with Jesus' baptism and concluding with the resurrection. It's also the shortest of the four gospels.

Key Verse

"Anyone who wants to be first must be the very last, and the servant of all" (Mark 9:35).

Luke

Time/Place

This gospel was written about AD 60–62 by Luke, a gentile missionary-doctor and colleague of the apostle Paul (Col. 4:14).

The Book

As the most *historical* gospel, Luke provides a detailed account of the life and ministry of Jesus, demonstrating Jesus' character and virtue. Luke focuses on Jesus as the divine Son of Man.

Of the four gospels, Luke's is the longest, and also the one which tells us most about Jesus' birth and childhood. Luke begins his gospel with the birth of John the Baptist and concludes with the ascension of Jesus into heaven.

Key Verse

"For the Son of Man came to seek and save the lost" (Luke 19:10).

John

Time/Place

This gospel was written by John, who, along with Peter and James, was part of the "inner circle" of Jesus' disciples (Matt. 4:21). It was written in the later part of the first century AD.

The Book

As the most *theological* gospel, John focuses on Jesus as the Son of God incarnate.

John begins his gospel by explaining that Jesus is the divine Word made flesh. This book contains lengthy teachings of Jesus and detailed miracle accounts (some not found in the other gospels). John concludes with Jesus' resurrection appearances.

Key Verse

"For God so loved the world that he gave his one and only Son, that whoever believes in him shall not perish but have eternal life" (John 3:16).

Harmony of the Gospels

Over the centuries, people have created many different harmonies to bring together all the events and teachings of the life of Jesus in the four gospels. The earliest harmonies date all the way back to Justin Martyr and Tatian in the second century AD.

One common type of harmony is a chronological harmony, also called a sequential harmony. This kind of harmony attempts to arrange the events of Jesus' life in the order that they happened. Putting the gospel stories into precise chronological order is a challenging task, primarily because ancient biographies have important differences from biographies written today. One main difference is historical sequencing. Modern biographies place a premium on historical sequencing. This means that the events of a person's life are typically narrated in the order in which they occurred. The biography usually begins with the person's birth and ends with his or her death, with the events in between presented chronologically. Ancient biographers, however, had a general commitment to the historical sequence, but they didn't feel the need to place every event in their writings in chronological order. Much more emphasis was given to developing an accurate picture of the person's character. Actions, events, and sayings were placed in the biographical story line to illustrate the person's character, no matter when they occurred.

Let's look at an example from the gospels: the story of a woman anointing Jesus' feet.

♦ John identifies the woman as Mary (Martha's sister) and places this event just before Jesus' triumphal entry into Jerusalem (John 12:1–8).

♦ Matthew and Mark also describe the same anointing as John, but don't mention the name of the woman. They place the story later in their gospels after they've told the story of Jesus' triumphal entry (Matt. 26:6–13; Mark 14:3–9).

♦ In Luke's gospel, there is also a story about a "sinful" woman anointing Jesus' feet, but Luke places this event much earlier in his gospel (Luke 7:36–50).

Was the anointing in Luke's gospel the same one as in Matthew, Mark, and John? If it's not the same event, this means there were two times a woman anointed Jesus' feet. If this was, however, the same anointing, it's possible that Luke placed this event out of historical sequence to illustrate what kind of Messiah Jesus was—the kind who heals and forgives. The two stories Luke writes just before the anointing story are ones of healing (Luke 7:1–17), and the anointing story is one of forgiveness (Luke 7:36–50).

Though we might not know the exact chronology of all gospel events, looking at the stories of Jesus together in a harmony can give us a fresh new perspective on the four gospels and the life and ministry of our Savior.

Event	Matt.	Mark	Luke	John
Gospel prologue			1:1–4	1:1–18
Genealogy of Jesus	1:1–17		3:23–38	
BIRTH and CHILDHOOD *Key Places: Bethlehem, Jerusalem, Egypt, Nazareth*				
Angel tells Zechariah that his wife Elizabeth will bear a son.			1:5–25	
Angel tells Mary that she will bear a son through the Holy Spirit.			1:26–38	
Mary visits Elizabeth; Mary's song.			1:39–56	
John the Baptist is born to Elizabeth and Zechariah.			1:57–80	
Angel tells Joseph in a dream to take Mary as his wife.	1:18–25			
Jesus is born in Bethlehem.			2:1–7	
Shepherds visit Jesus after angels appear to them.			2:8–20	
As an infant, Jesus is brought to the temple for dedication.			2:21–38	
Magi from the east visit Jesus.	2:1–12			
Joseph, Mary, and Jesus flee to Egypt to escape King Herod.	2:13–18			
Joseph, Mary, and Jesus return to Nazareth.	2:19–23		2:39–40	
At age twelve, Jesus amazes teachers at the temple.			2:41–52	
EARLY MINISTRY *Key Places: Jordan River, Judea, Cana, Jerusalem, Samaria*				
John the Baptist preaches in the Judean wilderness.	3:1–12	1:1–8	3:1–18	1:19–34
John baptizes Jesus in the Jordan River.	3:13–17	1:9–11	3:21–22	
Jesus resists Satan's temptations in the wilderness.	4:1–11	1:12–13	4:1–13	
Jesus gathers his first disciples.				1:35–51
Jesus turns water into wine at a wedding in Cana.				2:1–12
Cleansing of the temple in Jerusalem at Passover.				2:13–25
Nicodemus and Jesus converse.				3:1–21
John the Baptist testifies about Jesus.				3:22–36
Herod Antipas imprisons John the Baptist.			3:19–20	
Jesus meets the Samaritan woman at the well.				4:1–42
MINISTRY PRIMARILY in GALILEE *Key Places: Capernaum, Caesarea Philippi, Tyre/Sidon, Cana, Nain, Bethsaida*				
Jesus preaches throughout Galilee.	4:12–17, 23–25	1:14–15	4:14–15	4:43–45
In Cana, Jesus heals an official's son who is in Capernaum.				4:46–54
Jesus calls disciples.	4:18–22	1:16–20	5:1–11	

Event	Matt.	Mark	Luke	John
Jesus orders an impure spirit out of a man.		1:21–28	4:31–37	
Jesus heals Peter's mother-in-law and others.	8:14–17	1:29–39	4:38–44	
Jesus heals a man with leprosy.	8:1–4	1:40–45	5:12–16	
Jesus heals and forgives a paralyzed man.	9:1–8	2:1–12	5:17–26	
Jesus dines with sinners.	9:9–13	2:13–17	5:27–32	
People ask Jesus about fasting.	9:14–17	2:18–22	5:33–39	
Jesus heals a man at the pool of Bethesda on the Sabbath.				5:1–47
Pharisees accuse Jesus of Sabbath breaking.	12:1–14	2:23–3:6	6:1–11	
Large crowds seek out Jesus.	12:15–21	3:7–12	6:17–19	
Twelve disciples appointed.		3:13–19	6:12–16	
The Sermon on the Mount, including the Beatitudes, the Lord's Prayer, and the Golden Rule.	5:1–7:29		6:20–49; 11:1–13; 16:16–17	
In Cana, Jesus heals a centurion's servant.	8:5–13		7:1–10	
In Nain, Jesus raises a widow's son from the dead.			7:11–17	
From prison, John the Baptist asks if Jesus is the Messiah.	11:1–19		7:18–35	
Woes for the unrepentant; rest for those who come to Jesus.	11:20–30			
A "sinful" woman anoints Jesus.			7:36–50	
Pharisees accuse Jesus of being in league with Satan.	12:22–37	3:20–30	11:14–28	
Jesus predicts his own death; the sign of Jonah.	12:38–45		11:29–32	
Jesus' mother and brothers come to see him.	12:46–50	3:31–35	8:19–21	
Jesus teaches in parables.	13:1–52	4:1–34	8:1–18; 13:18–21	
Jesus calms a storm on the Sea of Galilee.	8:23–27	4:35–41	8:22–25	
Jesus casts demons out of a man and into pigs.	8:28–34	5:1–20	8:26–39	
Jesus raises Jairus's daughter and heals a woman who touches his cloak.	9:18–26	5:21–43	8:40–56	
Jesus heals blind men and a mute man.	9:27–34			
Jesus is rejected in his hometown.	13:53–58	6:1–6	4:16–30	
Jesus commissions the twelve disciples.	9:35–10:42	6:7–13	9:1–6	
Herod Antipas executes John the Baptist.	14:1–12	6:14–29	9:7–9	
Jesus feeds 5,000 people with five loaves and two fish.	14:13–21	6:30–44	9:10–17	6:1–15
Jesus walks on water on the Sea of Galilee.	14:22–36	6:45–56		6:16–21
Jesus teaches about the true bread from heaven.				6:22–71
Jesus teaches about inner vs. outer cleanliness.	15:1–20	7:1–23		

Event	Matt.	Mark	Luke	John
Jesus heals a woman's daughter in Tyre/Sidon.	15:21–28	7:24–30		
Jesus heals a deaf and mute man.		7:31–37		
Jesus feeds 4,000 people with seven loaves and a few fish.	15:29–39	8:1–10		
Pharisees and Sadducees ask Jesus for a sign.	16:1–12	8:11–21		
Jesus heals a blind man at Bethsaida.		8:22–26		
Peter calls Jesus the Messiah/Christ.	16:13–20	8:27–30	9:18–21	
Jesus predicts his death and resurrection.	16:21–28	8:31–9:1	9:22–27	
Transfiguration of Jesus.	17:1–13	9:2–13	9:28–36	
Jesus heals a demon-possessed boy.	17:14–20 (v. 21*)	9:14–29	9:37–43	
Again, Jesus predicts his death and resurrection.	17:22–23	9:30–32	9:44–45	
Teachings about temple tax, children, greatness, mercy.	17:24–18:35	9:33–50	9:46–50	
MINISTRY in JUDEA and PEREA *Key Places: Jerusalem, Bethany, Jericho*				
Jesus heads south toward Jerusalem.	19:1–2	10:1	9:51–56	7:1–14
The cost of following Jesus.	8:18–22		9:57–62	
Jesus teaches in the temple.				7:15–52
Jesus spares a woman who was caught in adultery.				7:53–8:11*
Disputes with Pharisees at the temple.				8:12–58
Jesus sends out the seventy-two.			10:1–24	
Parable of the good Samaritan.			10:25–37	
Jesus visits the home of Martha and Mary.			10:38–42	
Jesus pronounces judgment upon a wicked generation.			11:14–54	
Teachings about courage, true riches, recognizing the times.			12:1–13:9	
Jesus heals a crippled woman on the Sabbath.			13:10–17	
Jesus heals a man born blind.				9:1–41
Jesus says he is the Good Shepherd.				10:1–21
Some try to kill Jesus for blasphemy.				10:22–42
Teachings about entering the kingdom of God.			13:22–30	
Jesus mourns over Jerusalem.	23:37–39		13:31–35	
Jesus dines with Pharisees; heals a man with dropsy.			14:1–24	
Jesus tells large crowds what it means to follow him.			14:25–35	
Parables of lost sheep, lost coin, lost son (prodigal son).	18:12–14		15:1–32	

Event	Matt.	Mark	Luke	John
Parable of the shrewd manager.			16:1–15	
The story of Lazarus and the rich man.			16:19–31	
Teachings about forgiveness, faith, and duty.			17:1–10	
In Bethany, Jesus raises Lazarus from the dead.				11:1–44
Sanhedrin plots to kill Jesus in Jerusalem.				11:45–57
Ten men with leprosy healed; only one thanks Jesus.			17:11–19	
Teachings about the coming of the kingdom and last days.			17:20–37	
Parable of the persistent widow.			18:1–8	
Parable of the Pharisee and tax collector.			18:9–14	
Teachings about divorce.	19:1–12	10:2–12	16:18	
Teachings about children.	19:13–15	10:13–16	18:15–17	
Jesus tells a rich young ruler to give his wealth to the poor.	19:16–30	10:17–31	18:18–30	
Parable of the vineyard workers.	20:1–16			
Jesus again predicts his death and resurrection.	20:17–19	10:32–34	18:31–34	
James and John ask for positions of honor.	20:20–28	10:35–45		
Jesus heals Bartimaeus and another blind man in Jericho.	20:29–34	10:46–52	18:35–43	
Jesus visits Zacchaeus, a chief tax collector in Jericho.			19:1–27	
Mary anoints Jesus with expensive perfume in Bethany.	26:6–13	14:3–9		12:1–11
JESUS' LAST WEEK *Key Places: Jerusalem, Bethany, Mount of Olives, Temple Courts, Golgotha*				
Sunday				
Jesus' triumphal entry into Jerusalem riding on a donkey.	21:1–11	11:1–11	19:28–44	12:12–19
Monday				
Cleansing of the temple.	21:12–16	11:15–19	19:45–46	
Jesus again predicts his death.				12:20–50
Tuesday				
A fig tree withers after Jesus had cursed it.	21:17–22	11:12–14, 20–25		
Teachings about entering God's kingdom.	21:23–22:14	11:27–12:12	19:47–20:19	
Pharisees try to challenge Jesus, but Jesus challenges them.	22:15–33, 41–46	12:13–27, 35–40	20:20–47	
Greatest Commandment: Love God and love others.	22:34–40	12:28–34		
Teachings about hypocrisy.	23:1–36			

Event	Matt.	Mark	Luke	John
Widow puts two mites/coins into the temple treasury.		12:41–44	21:1–4	
On the Mount of Olives, Jesus teaches about the last days.	24:1–25:46	13:1–37	21:5–38	
Wednesday				
Judas Iscariot agrees to betray Jesus for thirty pieces of silver.	26:1–5, 14–16	14:1–2, 10–11	22:1–6	
Thursday				
Jesus washes the disciples' feet.				13:1–17
Jesus shares the Last Supper with his disciples.	26:17–30	14:12–26	22:7–30	13:18–30
Jesus predicts Peter's denials.	26:31–35	14:27–31	22:31–38	13:31–38
Teachings about vine/branches, Holy Spirit, and the world.				14:1–16:33
Jesus prays for believers.				17:1–26
Jesus prays in the garden of Gethsemane.	26:36–46	14:32–42	22:39–46	
Friday				
Judas betrays Jesus, and Jesus is arrested (after midnight).	26:47–56	14:43–52	22:47–53	18:1–12
Jesus stands trial before Annas, Caiaphas, and the Sanhedrin.	26:57–68	14:53–65	22:54	18:13–14, 19–24
Peter disowns Jesus three times, then weeps bitterly.	26:69–75	14:66–72	22:54–62	18:15–18, 25–27
Sanhedrin condemns Jesus (at daybreak).	27:1–2	15:1	22:63–71	
Judas hangs himself.	27:3–10			
Jesus stands trial before Pilate, then Herod Antipas, then back to Pilate who sentences Jesus.	27:11–26	15:2–15	23:1–25	18:28–19:16
Soldiers beat Jesus; put on him a crown of thorns and a robe.	27:27–31	15:16–20		19:1–3
Jesus is taken to Golgotha to be executed.	27:32	15:21	23:26–32	19:17
At Golgotha, Jesus is crucified between two thieves.	27:33–44	15:22–32	23:33–38	19:18–24
One thief believes in Jesus and asks to be remembered.			23:39–43	
Jesus entrusts his mother to John's care.				19:25–27
Jesus dies on the cross.	27:45–56	15:33–41	23:44–49	19:28–37
Joseph of Arimathea places Jesus' body in his own tomb (before sunset).	27:57–61	15:42–47	23:50–56	19:38–42
Saturday				
Roman guard is posted at the tomb.	27:62–66			

The gospels don't mention Wednesday specifically, but Luke 21:37–38 suggests that Jesus probably taught in the temple courts on this day. Judas and the religious leaders may have plotted together on this day.

Event	Matt.	Mark	Luke	John
Sunday				
Women find the stone rolled away from tomb, Jesus' body gone, and angels there.	28:1–8	16:1–8	24:1–8	20:1–2
Peter and John run to the empty tomb.			24:9–12	20:3–10
APPEARANCES and ASCENSION *Key Places: Jerusalem, Galilee, Emmaus*				
Jesus appears to Mary Magdalene and other women.	28:8–10	16:9–11*		20:11–18
Guards are bribed to say the disciples stole Jesus' body.	28:11–15			
Jesus appears to two disciples on the road to Emmaus.		16:12–13*	24:13–35	
Jesus appears to his disciples.		16:14*	24:36–49	20:19–23
Jesus appears to Thomas and other disciples.				20:24–31
Miracle of the fish at the Sea of Galilee.				21:1–14
Jesus restores Peter.				21:15–25
The Great Commission.	28:16–20	16:15–18*		
Jesus ascends into heaven forty days after his resurrection.		16:19–20*	24:50–53 (Acts 1:3–11)	

*Some early manuscripts do not have these verses.

Holy Land in the Time of Jesus

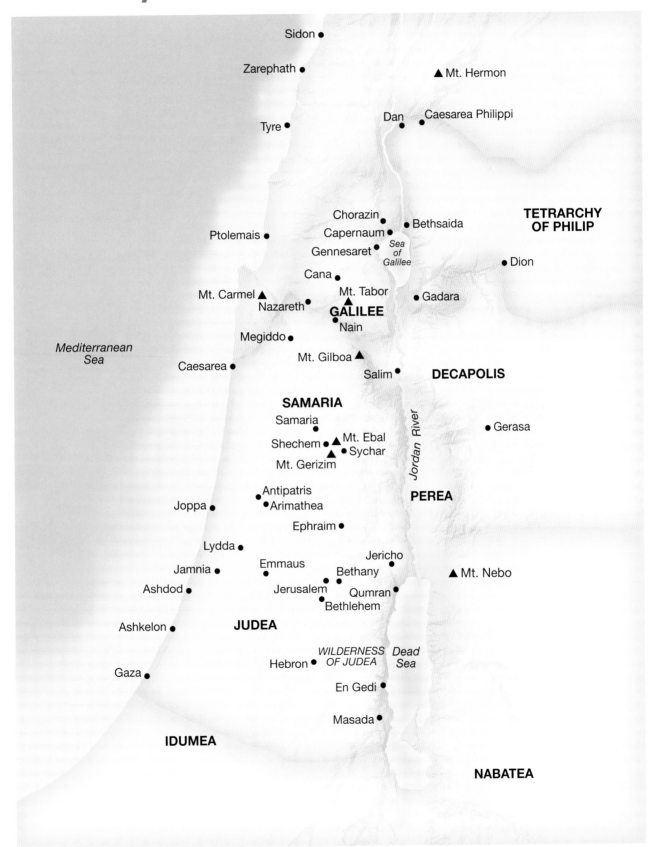

Genealogy of Jesus

THE GOSPEL OF LUKE

Luke lists the genealogy from Jesus to Adam.

Luke 3:23–38

Adam
Seth
Enosh
Kenan
Mahalalel
Jared
Enoch
Methuselah
Lamech
Noah
Shem
Arphaxad
Cainan
Shelah
Eber
Peleg
Reu
Serug
Nahor
Terah

THE GOSPEL OF MATTHEW

Matthew lists the genealogy from Abraham to Jesus.

Matt. 1:1–16

Abraham	**Abraham**
Isaac	Isaac
Jacob	Jacob
Judah and Tamar	Judah
Perez	Perez
Hezron	Hezron
Ram	Ram
Amminadab	Amminadab
Nahshon	Nahshon
Salmon and Rahab	Salmon
Boaz and Ruth	Boaz
Obed	Obed
Jesse	Jesse
King David and Uriah's wife	**David**

Solomon	**Nathan**
Rehoboam	Mattatha
Abijah	Menna
Asa	Melea
Jehoshaphat	Eliakim
Jehoram	Jonam
Uzziah	Joseph
Jotham	Judah
Ahaz	Simeon
Hezekiah	Levi
Manasseh	Matthat
Amon	Jorim
Josiah	Eliezer
Jeconiah	Joshua
	Er
	Elmadam
	Cosam
	Addi
	Melki
	Neri

Shealtiel	Shealtiel
Zerubbabel	**Zerubbabel**

Abihud	Rhesa
Eliakim	Joanan
Azor	Joda
Zadok	Josek
Akim	Semein
Elihud	Mattathias
Eleazar	Maath
Matthan	Naggai
Jacob	Esli
	Nahum
	Amos
	Mattathias
	Joseph
	Jannai
	Melki
	Levi
	Matthat
	Heli

Joseph and **Mary**	**Joseph**
JESUS	**JESUS**

Life of Jesus Time Line

Annunciation: Angel tells Mary she will bear a son through the Holy Spirit.
Lk 1:26–38

Birth of Christ: Jesus is born in Bethlehem.
Lk 2:1–7

4 BC

At the temple, Jesus is recognized as the Messiah.
Lk 2:21–38

Joseph, Mary, ar Jesus flee to Egy, to escape King Herod. They retur to Nazareth after Herod's death.
Mt 2:13–23

Angel tells Joseph to take Mary as his wife.
Mt 1:18–25

Shepherds visit Jesus lying in the manger.
Lk 2:8–20

Magi from the east visit Jesus.
Mt 2:1–12

"Today in the town of David a Savior has been born."
—LUKE 2:11

Pharisees accuse Jesus of being in league with Satan.
Mt 12:22–37; Mk 3:20–30; Lk 11:14–28

Jesus casts demons out of a man and into pigs.
Mt 8:28–34; Mk 5:1–20; Lk 8:26–39

Jesus feeds the 5,000.
Mt 14:13–21; Mk 6:30–44 Lk 9:10–17; Jn 6:1–15

Passover #3

Jesus raises a widow's son from the dead.
Lk 7:11–17

Jesus calms a storm on the Sea of Galilee.
Mt 8:23–27; Mk 4:35–41; Lk 8:22–25

Jesus raises Jairus's daughter and heals a woman who touches his cloak.
Mt 9:18–26; Mk 5:21–43; Lk 8:40–56

"This cup is the new covenant in my blood."
—LUKE 22:20

"Not my will, but yours be done." —LUKE 22:42

Last Supper: Jesus and disciples share a final meal.
Mt 26:17–30; Mk 14:12–26; Lk 22:7–30; Jn 13:18–30

Jesus prays in the garden of Gethsemane.
Mt 26:36–46; Mk 14:32–42; Lk 22:39–46

Judas Iscariot agrees to betray Jesus.
26:1–5, 14–16; 14:1–2, 10–11; 22:1–6

EDNESDAY**   THURSDAY

Passover #4

Midnight

Jesus washes his disciples' feet.
Jn 13:1–17

Jesus predicts Peter's denials.
Mt 26:31–35; Mk 14:27–31; Lk 22:31–38; Jn 13:31–38

Jesus is arrested when Judas betrays him.
Mt 26:47–56; Mk 14:43–52; Lk 22:47–53; Jn 18:1–12

"This same Jesus . . . will come back." —ACTS 1:11

Jesus appears to his disciples twice.
Mk 16:14*; Lk 24:36–49; Jn 20:19–31

Ascension
Mk 16:19–20*; Lk 24:50–53; Acts 1:3–11

Jesus appears to Mary Magdalene and other women.
Mt 28:8–10; Mk 16:9–11*; Jn 20:11–18

Jesus restores Peter: "Feed my sheep."
Jn 21:15–25

40 days after the Resurrection

Jesus appears to two men on the road to Emmaus.
Mk 16:12–13*; Lk 24:13–35

Jesus eats with his disciples after a miraculous catch of fish.
Jn 21:1–14

Great Commission: "Go and make disciples."
Mt 28:16–20

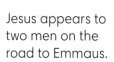

Time line dates are approximate.
* Some early manuscripts don't have these verses.
** The gospels don't mention Wednesday specifically, but Luke 21:37–38 suggests that Jesus taught in the temple courts on this day. Judas and the religious leaders may have plotted together on this day.

APPEARANCES & ASCENSION

"This is my Son, whom I love; with him I am well pleased." —MATTHEW 3:17

Baptism: John the Baptist baptizes Jesus.
Mt 3:13–17; Mk 1:9–11; Lk 3:21–22

Age 30; AD 27

First Miracle: Jesus turns water into wine.
Jn 2:1–12

"You must be born again." —JOHN 3:7

Nicodemus and Jesus converse.
Jn 3:1–21

Age 12

Jesus amazes teachers at the temple.
Lk 2:41–52

Jesus resists Satan's temptations in the wilderness.
Mt 4:1–11; Mk 1:12–13; Lk 4:1–13

Passover #1

First cleansing of the temple.
Jn 2:13–25

Jesus meets the Samaritan woman at the well.
Jn 4:1–42

"You are the Messiah, the Son of the Living God." —MATTHEW 16:16

Jesus teaches, "I am the bread of life."
Jn 6:22–71

Jesus feeds the 4,000.
Mt 15:29–39; Mk 8:1–10

Peter calls Jesus the Messiah/Christ.
Mt 16:13–20; Mk 8:27–30; Lk 9:18–21

Jesus walks on water.
Mt 14:22–36; Mk 6:45–56; Jn 6:16–21

Jesus heals a Canaanite woman's daughter.
Mt 15:21–28; Mk 7:24–30

Jesus heals a blind man at Bethsaida.
Mk 8:22–26

Transfiguration: Jesus is seen in glory.
Mt 17:1–13; Mk 9:2–13; Lk 9:28–36

Mary anoints Jesus' feet with perfume.
Mt 26:6–13; Mk 14:3–9; Jn 12:1–8

AD **30**

Second cleansing of the temple
Mt 21:12–16; Mk 11:15–19; Lk 19:45–46

Jesus commends the widow's offering.
Mk 12:41–44; Lk 21:1–4

Triumphal Entry: Jesus enters Jerusalem.
Mt 21:1–11; Mk 11:1–11; Lk 19:28–44; Jn 12:12–19

Pharisees and Jesus dispute in the temple courts.
Mt 22:15–45; Mk 12:13–27, 35–40; Lk 20:20–47

Olivet Discourse: Jesus teaches on the Mount of Olives.
Mt 24:1–25:46; Mk 13:1–37; Lk 21:5–38

"Hosanna in the highest heaven!" —Mark 11:10

"He is not here; he has risen." —Matthew 28:6

Jesus' body is placed in the tomb.
Mt 27:57–61; Mk 15:42–47; Lk 23:50–56; Jn 19:38–42

Crucifixion: Jesus is nailed to the cross.
Mt 27:33–44; Mk 15:22–32; Lk 23:33–38; Jn 19:18–24

Resurrection: Women find the tomb of Jesus empty.
Mt 28:1–8; Mk 16:1–8; Lk 24:1–8; Jn 20:1–2

9:00 a.m.   3:00 p.m.   Sunset

Simon is forced to carry Jesus' cross.
Mt 27:32; Mk 15:21; Lk 23:26–32; Jn 19:17

Jesus dies on the cross.
Mt 27:45–56; Mk 15:33–41; Lk 23:44–49; Jn 19:28–37

Roman guard is posted at the tomb.
Mt 27:62–66

Peter and John run to the tomb and find it empty.
Lk 24:9–12; Jn 20:3–10

"It is finished." —John 19:30

Jesus heals an official's son.
Jn 4:46–54

Jesus heals and forgives a paralyzed man.
Mt 9:1–8; Mk 2:1–12;
Lk 5:17–26

Jesus heals a man at the pool of Bethesda.
Jn 5:1–47

Passover #2

Jesus heals a centurion's servant.
Mt 8:5–13;
Lk 7:1–10

Jesus calls disciples.
Mt 4:18–22;
Mk 1:16–20;
Lk 5:1–11

Jesus dines with "sinners."
Mt 9:9–13;
Mk 2:13–17;
Lk 5:27–32

Sermon on the Mount: Jesus teaches with authority.
Mt 5:1–7:29; Lk 6:20–49;
11:1–13; 16:16–17

"Come, follow me."
—MATTHEW 4:19

"Do to others what you would have them do to you."
—MATTHEW 7:12

Jesus spares a woman caught in adultery.
Jn 7:53–8:11*

Jesus visits the home of Martha and Mary.
Lk 10:38–42

Jesus heals a man born blind.
Jn 9:1–41

Jesus mourns over Jerusalem.
Mt 22:37–39;
Lk 13:31–35

Jesus sends out the 72.
Lk 10:1–24

Jesus heals a crippled woman on the Sabbath.
Lk 13:10–17

Opponents try to stone Jesus for blasphemy.
Jn 10:22–42

Jesus dines with Pharisees and heals a man with dropsy.
Lk 14:1–24

Sanhedrin plots to kill Jesus.
Jn 11:45–57

Jesus heals Bartimaeus and another blind man.
Mt 20:29–34; Mk 10:46–52; Lk 18:35–43

Jesus raises Lazarus from the dead.
Jn 11:1–44

Rich young ruler and Jesus converse.
Mt 19:16–30; Mk 10:17–31; Lk 18:18–30

Jesus visits Zacchaeus the tax collector.
Lk 19:1–27

"All things are possible with God." —MARK 10:27

Jesus stands trial before Annas, Caiaphas, and the Sanhedrin.
Mt 26:57–68; Mk 14:53–65; Lk 22:54; Jn 18:13–14, 19–24

FRIDAY

Sanhedrin condemns Jesus.
Mt 27:1–2; Mk 15:1; Lk 22:63–71

Soldiers beat Jesus and mock him with a crown of thorns.
Mt 27:27–31; Mk 15:16–20; Jn 19:1–3

Daybreak

Peter disowns Jesus three times.
Mt 26:69–75; Mk 14:66–72; Lk 22:54–62; Jn 18:15–18, 25–27

Jesus stands trial before Herod and Pilate.
Mt 27:11–26; Mk 15:2–15; Lk 23:1–25; Jn 18:28–19:16

"Crucify him! Crucify him!" —LUKE 23:21

Parables of Jesus

Parable	Matthew	Mark	Luke
Lamp under a Bowl	5:14–16	4:21–22	8:16–17; 11:33–36
Wise and Foolish Builders	7:24–27		6:46–49
New Cloth on an Old Garment	9:16	2:21	5:36
New Wine in Old Wineskins	9:17	2:22	5:37–38
Sower and the Seeds	13:3–8, 18–23	4:3–8, 13–20	8:5–8, 11–15
Weeds in the Field	13:24–30, 36–43		
Mustard Seed	13:31–32	4:30–32	13:18–19
Yeast	13:33		13:20–21
Hidden Treasure	13:44		
Valuable Pearl	13:45–46		
Net of Good and Bad Fish	13:47–50		
Owner of a House	13:52		
Lost Sheep	18:12–14		15:4–7
Unmerciful Servant	18:23–35		
Workers in the Vineyard	20:1–16		
Two Sons	21:28–32		
Evil Tenants	21:33–44	12:1–11	20:9–18
Wedding Banquet	22:2–14		14:16–24
Fig Tree	24:32–35	13:28–31	21:29–33
Faithful vs. Wicked Servant	24:45–51		12:42–48
Ten Bridesmaids	25:1–13		
Talents	25:14–30		19:12–27
Sheep and Goats	25:31–46		
Growing Seed		4:26–29	
Watchful Servants		13:32–37	12:35–40
Money Lender			7:41–43
Good Samaritan			10:30–37
Friend in Need			11:5–8
Rich Fool			12:16–21
Unfruitful Fig Tree			13:6–9
Lowest Seat at the Feast			14:7–14
Cost of Discipleship			14:28–33
Lost Coin			15:8–10
Prodigal Son			15:11–32
Shrewd Manager			16:1–13
Rich Man and Lazarus			16:19–31
Master and His Servant			17:7–10
Persistent Widow			18:2–8
Pharisee and Tax Collector			18:9–14

The Risen Savior

From Palm Sunday to Resurrection Sunday

During his three-year ministry, Jesus made (and accepted) extraordinary claims about himself. When asked point-blank if he was "the Messiah, the Son of God," Jesus answered affirmatively (Matt. 26:63–64). He declared himself and God "one"—a statement that outraged his Jewish listeners. They considered such words blasphemous and they almost stoned Jesus on the spot (John 10:30–33). Jesus had to know that such claims would cost him his life. In fact, he told his disciples exactly what would happen to him: "We are going up to Jerusalem, and the Son of Man will be delivered over to the chief priests and the teachers of the law. They will condemn him to death and will hand him over to the Gentiles to be mocked and flogged and crucified" (Matt. 20:18–19). Yet he headed to Jerusalem, straight to the cross that awaited him there— knowingly, willingly, and sacrificially.

Journey to the Cross

Matthew 21–27; Mark 11–15; Luke 19–23; John 12–19

Starting with Jesus' arrival in Jerusalem, all four gospels focus extensively on his final week—a third of Matthew, a third of Mark, a fourth of Luke, and nearly half of John.

Jesus' triumphal entry into Jerusalem on what has come to be known as Palm Sunday raised the crowd's messianic hopes yet again. He rode into Jerusalem on a donkey, fulfilling the prophecy of Zechariah 9:9: "See, your king comes to you, righteous and victorious, lowly and riding on a donkey, on a colt, the foal of a donkey." With palm branches in hand, people lined the road shouting *hosanna,* which means "salvation

at last!" Surely this was the moment, many assumed. But then, people noticed Jesus was weeping, not waving a sword (Luke 19:41)— hardly the behavior of a conquering king.

What followed this event was a strange, turbulent week.

On Monday, Jesus moved through the temple courts, angrily turning over the tables of corrupt money changers and merchants.

On Tuesday, his disruptive acts from the day before prompted fierce arguments with the religious leaders at the temple. Later, on the Mount of Olives east of Jerusalem, Jesus prepared his followers for his departure. Jesus told them about the coming signs of the end times, his glorious return, and the ultimate triumph of God's kingdom.

The gospels don't specifically mention what happened on Wednesday, but we do know that sometime during the week the religious leaders plotted against Jesus. They also found a willing coconspirator in Judas Iscariot, one of Jesus' twelve disciples. Judas accepted thirty pieces of silver from the chief priests in exchange for handing Jesus over to the authorities.

On Thursday night, Jesus gathered his closest followers in an upstairs room to share the Passover meal one final time with them. He used the occasion to institute a new meal—the Lord's Supper. This meal would commemorate his body broken and his blood spilled as a sacrifice. Jesus explained to his disciples, "This is my blood of the covenant, which is poured out for many for the forgiveness of sins" (Matt. 26:27–28). Before the gathering concluded, Judas slipped out of the room in order to carry out his plan to betray Jesus.

Just after that last supper with his disciples, Jesus went to the garden of Gethsemane with Peter, James, and John to pray. Jesus was visibly in deep anguish as he contemplated the horrific death he would soon face. "He prayed more earnestly, and his sweat was like drops of blood falling to the ground" (Luke 22:44). While his closest disciples slept, Jesus wrestled in prayer—alone, prostrate, drenched in a bloody sweat. Through prayer, he was given strength to carry out the Father's plan: "Father, if you are willing, take this cup from me; yet not my will, but yours be done" (Luke 22:42). Strengthened with holy resolve, he rose, just in time to meet Judas and the mob that had come to arrest him.

In the wee hours of Friday morning, the Jewish and Roman authorities sent Jesus to illegal nighttime trials. Pontius Pilate, who was the Roman prefect of Judea, sentenced Jesus to death.

Jesus was stripped and flogged mercilessly by Roman soldiers skilled in the brutal business of execution. The men took turns punching him, spitting on him, and mocking him with a purple robe and a crown of thorns. Then they led him to Golgotha—an infamous execution site, along a major thoroughfare outside the city walls—where they hammered him to a cross. Between two convicted criminals, Jesus died a gruesome, agonizing death. Yet even then, while on the cross, Jesus prayed for his executioners: "Father, forgive them, for they do not know what they are doing" (Luke 23:34).

Shortly before the beginning of the Sabbath day, which started at sunset on Friday, the Roman soldiers overseeing the crucifixion realized that Jesus was already dead. (Death by crucifixion could sometimes take days.) The soldiers removed his lifeless body from the cross and, on the orders of Pilate, released it to Joseph of Arimathea, a wealthy member of the Sanhedrin who had come to believe in Jesus. Joseph wrapped Christ's body in "a clean linen cloth, and placed it in his own new tomb that he had cut out of the rock" (Matt. 27:59–60). Joseph, with the help of Nicodemus and probably others too, rolled a big stone over the mouth of the tomb.

At the request of the Jewish leaders, Pilate sent soldiers to put an official Roman seal on the tomb and stand guard there, lest followers of Jesus "come and steal the body" and tell everyone that Jesus had risen from the dead (Matt. 27:64).

The Flagellation of Our Lord Jesus Christ by William Adolphe Bouguereau, 1880

Journey to the Cross

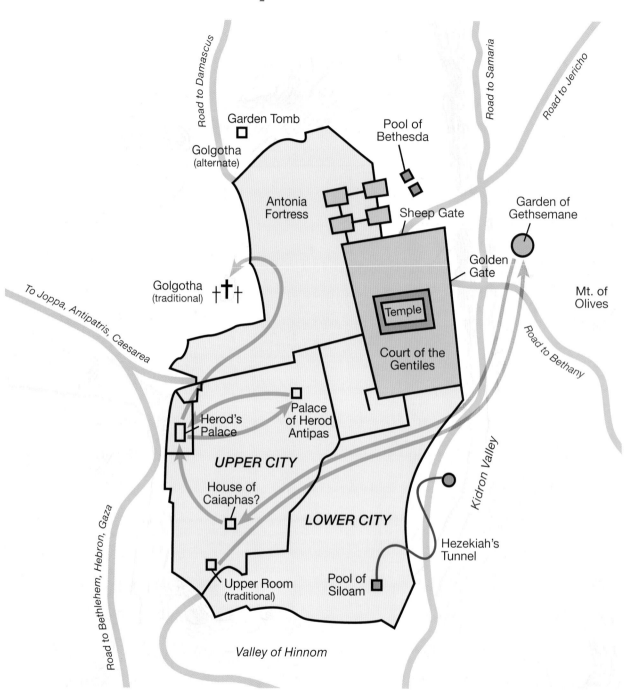

1. After the Last Supper in the upper room, Jesus prays in the garden of Gethsemane, where he is also arrested. Luke 22:12; Matt. 26:36; Mark 14:32

2. Jesus stands trial before Annas (location unknown), then Caiaphas and the Sanhedrin at the house of Caiaphas. John 18:13, 24; Matt. 26:57; Mark 14:53; Luke 22:54

3. Jesus stands trial before Pilate at Herod's Palace. Matt. 27:2; Mark 15:1; Luke 23:1; John 18:28

4. Pilate sends Jesus to Herod Antipas, who sends Jesus back to Pilate. Luke 23:7, 11

5. Jesus is crucified at Golgotha. Matt. 27:33; Mark 15:22; Luke 23:33; John 19:17

Jesus' Hours on the Cross

K One of the criminals who hung there hurled insults at Jesus: "Aren't you the Christ? Save yourself and us!" **Lk 23:39**

L But the other criminal rebuked him … Then he said, "Jesus, remember me when you come into your kingdom." **Lk 23:40, 42**

O At the sixth hour darkness came over the whole land until the ninth hour. **Mk 15:33**

J The soldiers also came up and mocked him … "If you are the king of the Jews, save yourself." **Lk 23:36-37**

M Jesus answered him, "I tell you the truth, today you shall be with me in paradise." **Lk 23:43**

I The chief priests mockingly said, "He saved others … but he can't save himself!" **Mk 15:31**

N Jesus … said to his mother, "Dear woman, here is your son," and to the disciple, "Here is your mother." **Jn 19:26-27**

Jesus cried … "My God, my God, why have you forsaken me?" **Mt 27:46** **P**

H Those who passed by hurled insults at him … saying … "Come down from the cross, if you are the Son of God!" **Mt 27:39-40**

G The soldiers divided up his clothes and cast lots to see what each would get. **Mk 15:24**

Jesus said, "Father, forgive them, for they do not know what they are doing." **Lk 23:34**

It was the third hour when they crucified him. **Mk 15:25**

ROMAN (and Modern) EXPRESSION OF TIME

JEWISH EXPRESSION OF TIME

"I am thirsty." **Q** Jn 19:28

"It is finished." **R** Jn 19:30

"Father, into your hands I commit my spirit." **S** Lk 23:46

THE CRUCIFIXION

9 AM — 3rd hour

F Crucified **Lk 23:33**

E Led to Calvary **Lk 23:26**

D Sentenced **Lk 23:23-24**

C Returned to Pilate **Lk 23:11**

B Sent to Herod **Lk 23:6-10**

A Before Pilate **Mk 15:1**

↑

START HERE

JESUS DIES

9th hour — **3 PM**

EVENTS IMMEDIATELY FOLLOWING

T The earthquake and tearing in two of the curtain (veil) **Mt 27:51**

U Tombs break open **Mt 27:52**

V The centurion … exclaimed, "Surely he was the Son of God." **Mt 27:54**

W The confession of the multitude **Lk 23:48**

X The thieves' legs are broken **Jn 19:31-32**

Y The soldier pierces Jesus' side **Jn 19:34**

Z The burial **Jn 19:38-42** The tomb is secured by a seal and a guard is posted **Mt 27:66**

EVENTS PRECEDING

1 The Last Supper **Lk 22:14**
2 Gethsemane **Mt 26:36**
3 The arrest **Jn 18:12**
4 At the house of Caiaphas **Lk 22:54**

Thin lines indicate sequence of events only. Exact times are not recorded in Scripture.

Only Mark's Gospel states actual times— "3rd hour," "6th hour," "9th hour".

©Hugh Claycombe

141

The Empty Tomb

Matthew 28; Mark 16; Luke 24; John 20–21

Early Sunday morning, several women who had been followers of Jesus arrived at his tomb, hoping for an opportunity to properly anoint his body. (The start of the Sabbath on Friday evening had kept them from being able to perform this customary burial act.) What they found in the tomb left them shocked, stunned, and bewildered, but ultimately overjoyed.

The tomb was open and empty! Grave linens were lying loose. Angels appeared, saying matter-of-factly, "He is not here; he has risen, just as he said" (Matt. 28:6). And then, the followers of Jesus, both singly and in groups, had actual encounters with the resurrected Jesus—not a phantom or a spirit, but a back-from-the-dead Savior they could touch.

The gospel accounts of the resurrection are chaotic and hard to piece together. And why would we expect anything else? People were running, telling others, weeping, trembling, feeling fearful and joyful, and doubting and worshiping (John 20:4, 11; Mark 16:8; Matt. 28:8, 17).

Skeptics have offered all sorts of theories for what they think really happened. Obviously, the disciples stole the body, they say. Or the women got confused and went to the wrong tomb. Or perhaps Jesus never actually died on the cross, but only appeared to be dead. Then, in the cool air of the tomb, he resuscitated, pushed the huge stone away, overpowered the guards, escaped, and conspired with his followers to pull off the greatest ruse in history.

None of these scenarios are remotely plausible. And certainly, none of these theories can account for the transformed lives of the disciples. Consider this: in the garden of Gethsemane, when Jesus had willingly surrendered to the authorities without a fight, his little band of close disciples disintegrated. When pressed, his disciple Peter had sworn that he didn't even know Jesus. Just a few followers at that moment, mostly women, had watched the crucifixion from a safe distance. To Jesus' followers, it was over; the life of their teacher, their Messiah, the movement he'd started—all over.

Only, it wasn't.

Something unprecedented and cataclysmic happened early on Sunday morning. In the dim light of day, a timid, demoralized group

The Three Marys at the Tomb
by William Adolphe Bouguereau, 1876

of disciples morphed into a fearless band of witnesses. In just a few weeks' time, Peter went from angrily telling a servant girl that he didn't even know Jesus to standing in front of the same powerful men who had sentenced his master to death, boldly insisting that Jesus was the Messiah, was alive, and was the only means of salvation. What can explain this, other than the truth of the resurrection of their Savior?

His Promise to Come Again

Mark 16; Luke 24; Acts 1

About six weeks after the crucifixion, the resurrected Christ gathered his disciples one final time and told them their mission—the Great Commission: "Go and make disciples of all nations, baptizing them in the name of the Father and of the Son and of the Holy Spirit" (Matt. 28:19). Then they watched wide-eyed as he rose into heaven. As they stood there staring, angels told them, "Men of Galilee . . . why do you stand here looking into the sky? This same Jesus, who has been taken from you into heaven, will come back in the same way you have seen him go into heaven" (Acts 1:11).

That message wasn't only for a handful of disciples in Galilee two millennia ago. That message is for all believers in Jesus— then, now, and in the future. Believers in Jesus wait and watch eagerly for his return because he will "come at an hour when you do not expect him" (Matt. 24:44).

But while his followers wait, there's work to do. Jesus said, "The work of God is this: to believe in the one he has sent" (John 6:29).

We're called to put our trust in everything that the Bible reveals about Jesus: that he was and is the eternal Son of God, both fully God and fully human; that he lived a perfect life of trust and obedience; that on the cross Jesus willingly offered his life as a payment for the sins of the world; that he was our sacrificial substitute, taking our sins—and God's just punishment for those sins—upon himself; that he grants forgiveness and gives new, eternal, abundant life to all who put their faith in him. As John 3:16—perhaps the most well-known verse in the Bible—says: "For God so loved the world that he gave his one and only Son, that whoever believes in him shall not perish but have eternal life."

The Ascension by John Singleton Copley, 1775

143

Prophecies Fulfilled by Jesus

Prophecy	Old Testament	New Testament
Fulfill God's promise to dwell among his people.	Zech. 2:10	John 1:14
Be a son who is given.	Isa. 9:6	John 3:16
Be a descendant of Abraham.	Gen. 17:7	Matt. 1:1
Be of the tribe of Judah.	Gen. 49:8–10	Matt. 1:1–3
Be born a king in the line of King David.	Isa. 9:7	Matt. 1:1; Luke 1:32–33
Be called *Immanuel*—God with us.	Isa. 7:14	Matt. 1:22–23
Be born of a virgin.	Isa. 7:14	Matt. 1:18; Luke 1:27
Be born in the town of Bethlehem of Judah (Judea).	Mic. 5:2	Matt. 2:1–6
Be a firstborn son who is consecrated (set apart).	Num. 8:17	Luke 2:7, 22–23
Receive gifts from kings and be bowed down to.	Ps. 72:10–11	Matt. 2:1–2, 11
Be called out of Egypt.	Hos. 11:1	Matt. 2:13–15
His way prepared by a messenger sent in the spirit of Elijah.	Isa. 40:3; Mal. 3:1; 4:5	Matt. 11:13–14; Luke 3:3–4; 7:27
Have God's Spirit upon him.	Isa. 11:2	Luke 3:21–22
Anointed to proclaim freedom for the captives.	Isa. 61:1	Luke 4:16–21
Minister in Zebulun and Naphtali (Galilee).	Isa. 9:1–2	Matt. 4:12–14
Fulfill the promises (covenant) to Israel and be a light to the gentiles.	Isa. 42:6	Luke 2:28–32
Be a light for the nations.	Isa. 60:1–3	John 12:46
Be a healer.	Isa. 29:18; 35:5	Matt. 11:4–5
Care for the needy.	Ps. 72:12–14	Luke 7:22
Be a prophet like Moses.	Deut. 18:15–19	John 6:14; 7:40
Have eternal existence.	Mic. 5:2	John 1:1–2; 8:58
Take up our pain and bear our suffering.	Isa. 53:4	Matt. 8:16–17
Be a servant of God.	Isa. 42:1	Matt. 12:16–18
Speak in parables with hidden meaning.	Ps. 78:2	Matt. 13:34–35
Some people's hearts will be calloused toward him.	Isa. 6:9–10	Matt. 13:13–15
Have great zeal for God's house (the temple).	Ps. 69:9	John 2:13–17
Be the Good Shepherd who cares for his sheep.	Isa. 40:11	John 10:11

Prophecy	Old Testament	New Testament
Come to Jerusalem as the king, riding on a donkey.	Zech. 9:9	Matt. 21:1–7
Make a new covenant.	Jer. 31:31–34	Luke 22:15–20
Be hated without reason.	Ps. 35:19	John 15:24–25
Be rejected as the capstone (cornerstone).	Ps. 118:22–23	Matt. 21:42
Be sold for thirty pieces of silver.	Zech. 11:12	Matt. 26:14–15
Be betrayed by a friend.	Pss. 41:9; 55:12–14	Matt. 26:23–25
Be the shepherd struck and his sheep scattered.	Zech. 13:7; Pss. 38:11; 88:18	Matt. 26:56; Mark 14:27
Be accused by false witnesses.	Ps. 27:12	Matt. 26:59–60
Be afflicted, but remain silent.	Isa. 53:7	Matt. 27:12; Luke 23:9
Be sinless.	Isa. 53:9	1 Peter 2:21–23
Be despised and rejected.	Isa. 53:3	Luke 17:25
Be beaten, struck, spat upon, and mocked.	Isa. 50:6; 52:14; Mic. 5:1	Matt. 26:67; 27:30; John 19:1–2
Be given gall and vinegar (sour wine) to drink.	Ps. 69:21–22	Matt. 27:34
Have his hands and feet pierced.	Ps. 22:16	John 20:25–27
Be lifted up, just as Moses lifted up the bronze serpent in the wilderness.	Num. 21:9	John 3:14–15
Take our punishment upon himself to bring peace and healing.	Isa. 53:4–5	Matt. 26:28; Mark 10:45
Soldiers cast lots for his clothing.	Ps. 22:18	John 19:23–24
Be thirsty during his execution.	Ps. 22:15	John 19:28
Feel forsaken by God.	Ps. 22:1	Matt. 27:46; Mark 15:34
Commit his spirit into God's hands.	Ps. 31:5	Luke 23:46
Be the Passover lamb—slain, a male without blemish, and no broken bones.	Ex. 12:3–7, 46	John 19:32–33; 1 Cor. 5:7; 1 Peter 1:19
Be pierced.	Zech. 12:10	John 19:34–37
Defeat Satan and break Satan's power.	Gen. 3:15	Heb. 2:14; 1 John 3:8
Be buried with the rich.	Isa. 53:9	Matt. 27:57–60
Be raised from the dead.	Pss. 16:8–10; 49:15; 86:13	Luke 24:6–8; Acts 2:29–32; 13:34
Be victorious over death.	Isa. 25:8	John 2:19–22; 1 Cor. 15:54

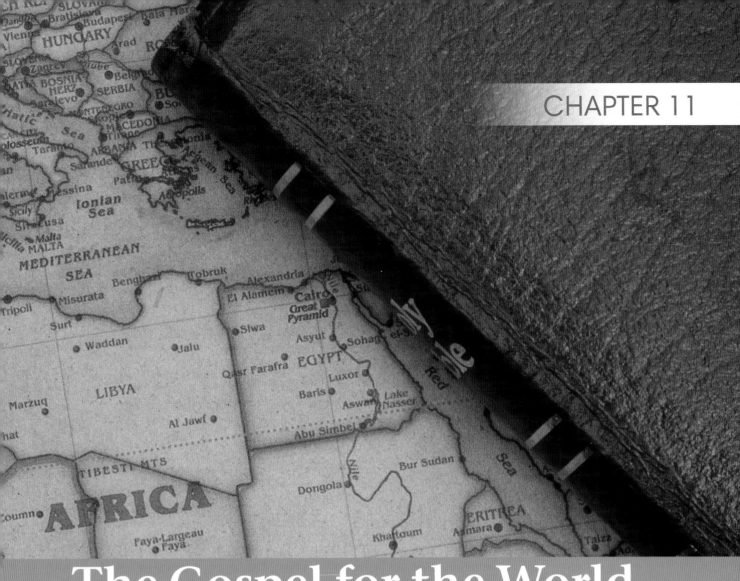

CHAPTER 11

The Gospel for the World

From Jerusalem to Rome
AD 30–60

The Holy Spirit at Pentecost

Apostles Peter and Paul

Book of Acts and Early Epistles

The resurrection of Christ changed everything. Whatever doubts the disciples might have had were erased. (Even "doubting Thomas" believed, declaring Christ to be "My Lord and my God!" John 20:28.) This is where the biblical narrative of the four gospels concludes. It's in the book of Acts (the sequel to the gospel of Luke) where we learn what happened next to the disciples—and to the whole world for that matter. In these stories, which occurred in the first thirty or so years after the resurrection, we see believers in Jesus be empowered by the Holy Spirit to take the good news (the *gospel*) of their risen Lord to a world in need of salvation.

The Holy Spirit at Pentecost

Acts 1–3

The story of Acts begins with Christ's ascension into heaven. Before he departed,

he told his closest disciples what would happen to them: "You will receive power when the Holy Spirit comes on you; and you will be my witnesses in Jerusalem, and in all Judea and Samaria, and to the ends of the earth" (Acts 1:8).

In this one Bible verse, we get the basic story line of Acts. *Who* will receive this power? "You"—all who are disciples of Jesus. *What* will they be empowered to do? "Be my witnesses"—testify about all they experienced with Jesus and share the gospel of God's forgiveness and love. *When* will this happen? "When the Holy Spirit comes." *Where* will this happen? Firstly, they'll be witnesses "in Jerusalem," then "Judea and Samaria," and they won't stop until they get "to the ends of the earth."

As instructed, the disciples got to work, praying and waiting in Jerusalem. But they didn't have to wait long. While Jews from all over were gathered in Jerusalem for the festival of Pentecost, the Holy Spirit of God came upon the followers of Jesus like a hurricane!

> Suddenly a sound like the blowing of a violent wind came from heaven and filled the whole house where they were sitting. They saw what seemed to be tongues of fire that separated and came to rest on each of them. All of them were filled with the Holy Spirit and began to speak in other tongues as the Spirit enabled them. (Acts 2:2–4)

The believers were empowered to share the truth of God with all those foreign visitors in languages that they themselves had never learned! The apostle Peter seized the moment and gave a short sermon to the crowd about Christ's death and resurrection. As a result, three thousand people repented of their sins, put their faith in Jesus, and were baptized.

This new spiritual community, called the church, was fiercely devoted to the apostles' teaching. They ate together and helped one another financially. They shared a common faith, a common life, and a common mission. They worshiped wholeheartedly, prayed fervently, and saw God do miraculous things through the apostles. As a result, the whole city of Jerusalem was in awe. More and more Jews believed in Jesus as the Messiah.

Persecution and the Church

Acts 4–9

Not surprisingly, this rapid, new movement was soon met with backlash. Peter and John were arrested and brought before the Sanhedrin, the same group that only weeks before had condemned Jesus to death (Matt. 26:59–68). Filled with the Holy Spirit, Peter was fearless! He boldly preached the gospel to them, declaring that "salvation is found in no one else" besides Jesus (Acts 4:12). He insisted that he and the apostles would never stop sharing this truth. It was just as Jesus had told them:

> When you are brought before synagogues, rulers and authorities, do not worry about how you will defend yourselves or what you will say, for the Holy Spirit will teach you at that time what you should say. (Luke 12:11–12)

Threatened and released, Peter and John ramped up their efforts to share the good news, and the church continued to grow. The more the Jewish leaders cracked down, the more the church spoke up. Nothing could

deter Christ's followers, not threats, floggings, or even death. One church leader, Stephen, was dragged outside Jerusalem and stoned to death for testifying about Jesus. Stephen's death sparked a wave of violent persecution against the church.

Believers in Jesus fled Jerusalem in droves. But ironically, this only meant that the gospel was advancing. Opposition in Jerusalem sent them into Judea and Samaria, just as Jesus had said would happen (Acts 1:8). Philip preached the gospel in Samaria and then to an Ethiopian man the Lord led him to on a road in Judea. The Ethiopian man trusted in Jesus and was immediately baptized. The road the man was on headed toward Gaza, a port city from where he'd presumably travel to Africa. The Great Commission Jesus had given his followers—"to make disciples of all nations"—was just beginning (Matt. 28:19).

The Release of St Peter by Bernardo Strozzi, c. 1635

One of the chief engineers of the persecution campaign against the church was a young man named Saul (also called Paul). About five years after Stephen was martyred in Jerusalem (Saul had been there for that; Acts 7:58; 8:1), Saul set his sights on Damascus, a city northeast of Jerusalem. He was headed to Damascus to arrest believers in Jesus who had fled the persecution in Jerusalem. Saul set out to apprehend followers of Jesus, but on the way, it was he who was "apprehended by Christ Jesus" (Phil. 3:12 KJV). A great light flashed from heaven, he fell to the ground, and the risen Lord revealed the truth: "I am Jesus, whom you are persecuting" (Acts 9:5). Physically blinded by the experience, Saul arrived in Damascus where the Lord directed a man named Ananias to go to him and restore his sight. Confronted, then converted by Jesus, Saul joined the very movement he had tried to abolish!

Peter's Mission

Acts 10–12

Meanwhile, God was using the apostle Peter to open the door of salvation—and of the church—to those outside the Jewish community. Until this point, the church consisted of mostly Jewish believers, and it

> ### ⟫ LUKE
>
> Luke was a gentile doctor who wrote the gospel of Luke and the book of Acts (Col. 4:14). He became a ministry colleague of the apostle Paul, traveling with him on his second and third missionary journeys, and his journey to Rome. Luke was also one of the last who remained with Paul during Paul's imprisonment in Rome just before his death (Acts 16:10; 2 Tim. 4:11).

was viewed by the Romans as a religious group within Judaism. Even some in the church, like Peter, didn't fully understand that the power of the gospel was for all people, no matter who they were in society or where they came from. So God sent Peter to the home of Cornelius, a Roman centurion and a gentile (non-Jew). There, Peter saw the Holy Spirit fill the gentile believers, and he was convinced: "I now realize how true it is that God does not show favoritism but accepts from every nation the one who fears him and does what is right" (Acts 10:34–35).

Soon, there was a growing and thriving community of gentile believers in Antioch of Syria (Acts 11:19–30). In fact, it was in this city that the followers of Jesus were first called *Christians*, and it was from here that Saul (Paul) began launching missionary efforts to reach the world with the gospel.

Paul's Journeys

Acts 13–28

About half of the chapters in Acts focus on Paul's journeys. For his first missionary outreach, Paul teamed up with Barnabas and for a short time with John Mark (thought to be the author of the gospel of Mark). By the Holy Spirit's leading, they took the gospel to the island of Cyprus, then to cities in the south-central region of Asia Minor (modern-day Turkey). Everywhere Paul went, it seemed there was either a riot or a revival—sometimes both! He typically visited local synagogues first, where he almost always encountered opposition. Next, he shared God's truth with gentiles, who were often more receptive.

On his second big missionary journey, Paul was accompanied by Silas, and they were later joined by Timothy, a husband-and-wife team Priscilla and Aquila, as well as Luke the author of the gospel of Luke and Acts. Paul headed north and then west through Asia Minor and Greece, this apostolic team strengthening believers and establishing churches everywhere they went.

On his third journey, Paul retraced his steps, revisiting cities he'd previously evangelized and church congregations he had helped plant. During a two-year layover in Ephesus, God did extraordinary things through Paul and many throughout the region came to faith. While on this mission, Paul wrote his longest epistle (letter) in the New Testament—the epistle to the Romans. This was Paul's magnum opus, his comprehensive explanation of God's plan of salvation.

Later, when Paul was in Jerusalem, he was falsely accused of defiling the temple, arrested, and sent to prison. He was held in prison two years awaiting trial. Nevertheless, he shared his faith with various high-ranking officials while he waited in chains. Paul was eventually put on a ship headed to Rome to appeal his case to

THE HOLY SPIRIT

The Bible teaches that the Spirit is involved in the works of God: creation (Gen. 1:2; Ps. 104:30); the incarnation of Jesus (Matt. 1:18; Luke 1:35); the resurrection (Rom. 1:4; 8:11); salvation (John 15:26; 16:8; Rom. 8:14–17); and the Christian life (John 16:13; Rom. 8:26–27; Gal. 5:22–23). The Spirit is a person: he can be lied to (Acts 5:3–4); he can be grieved (Eph. 4:30); and he has a name (Matt. 28:19). The Spirit is God (1 Cor. 3:16; 12:4–6; 2 Peter 1:21).

Caesar. This journey would be the farthest he had travelled—to Rome, the epicenter of the Greco-Roman world, far from where the church had begun in Jerusalem, Judea, and Samaria (Acts 1:8).

When he arrived in Rome, Paul was placed under house arrest to await yet another trial. This is where the narrative of Acts ends, with Paul using the difficult situation he was in as an opportunity to tell others about salvation in Jesus: "For two whole years Paul stayed there in his own rented house and welcomed all who came to see him. He proclaimed the kingdom of God and taught about the Lord Jesus Christ—with all boldness and without hindrance!" (Acts 28:30–31).

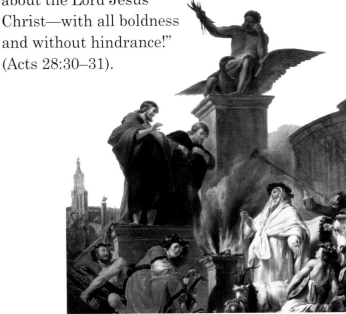

Paul and Barnabas at Lystra by Nicolaes Pieterszoon Berchem, 1650

Peter and Paul

These two men had very different spiritual journeys to Christ, but a common goal of spreading the gospel and glorifying God in every aspect of their lives.

Peter	Paul
Also called Simon and Cephas which means "the rock" (John 1:42).	Also called Saul, his Hebrew name; Paul is his Roman or Gentile name (Acts 13:9).
A Jew and fisherman from Capernaum in Galilee (Matt. 4:18; 8:5, 14).	A Jew and Roman citizen by birth from Tarsus in Cilicia (Acts 16:37–38; 21:39).
An "unschooled" man who was trained by Jesus (Acts 4:13).	Trained in the Scriptures by the famous Pharisee Gamaliel (Acts 22:3).
Married (Matt. 8:14).	Unmarried (1 Cor. 7:7–8).
Called by Jesus to be one of the twelve apostles (Matt. 4:18–20; 10:2).	Encountered Jesus on the road to Damascus (Acts 9:1–16). Became an "apostle to the Gentiles" (Gal. 2:8).
Denied knowing Jesus three times when Jesus was arrested (Luke 22:54–62).	Violently persecuted believers before his conversion (Acts 8:3).
Commissioned by the Lord to care for believers; "feed my sheep" (John 21:15–17).	Commissioned by the Lord to proclaim Jesus to gentiles, kings, and Israel (Acts 9:15).
Filled with the Holy Spirit at Pentecost in Jerusalem (Acts 2:4).	Filled with the Holy Spirit in Damascus (Acts 9:17).
Proclaimed Jesus as the Messiah (Matt. 16:16; Acts 2:36).	Proclaimed Jesus as the Messiah (Acts 17:3).
A leader of the church in Jerusalem (Acts 15:7).	Launched his missionary journeys from Antioch of Syria (Acts 13:1–3).
Performed miracles, exorcised evil spirits, and raised the dead (Acts 2:3–8; 5:16; 9:36–43).	Performed miracles, exorcised evil spirits, and raised the dead (Acts 14:8–10; 19:12; 20:9–12).
Received a vision about what "God has made clean" (Acts 10:9–16).	Received a vision of a man from Macedonia (Acts 16:9–10).
Imprisoned for his faith (Acts 12:3–5).	Imprisoned for his faith (Acts 24:27; 2 Tim. 1:16).
Wrote two epistles in the New Testament (1 and 2 Peter) and may have been the main source for the gospel of Mark.	Wrote thirteen epistles in the New Testament.
Martyred in Rome during Emperor Nero's persecution. According to tradition, he was crucified upside down.	Martyred in Rome during Emperor Nero's persecution. According to tradition, he was beheaded.
Jesus had said that even in the manner of his death, Peter would glorify God (John 21:19).	In his last epistle, Paul wrote, "My departure is near. I have fought the good fight, I have finished the race, I have kept the faith" (2 Tim. 4:6–7).

Paul's First Missionary Journey

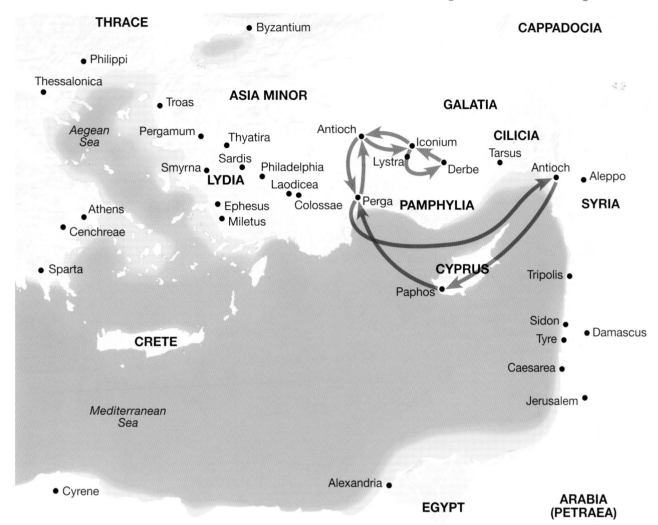

THRACE

• Byzantium

• Philippi

Thessalonica
•

CAPPADOCIA

ASIA MINOR

GALATIA

Aegean
Sea

• Troas

Pergamum •

Antioch

CILICIA

• Thyatira

• Iconium

Tarsus

Sardis

Lystra

•

• Derbe

Antioch

• Aleppo

Smyrna •

Philadelphia

• Laodicea

PAMPHYLIA

SYRIA

LYDIA

• Ephesus

• Colossae

• Perga

• Athens

• Miletus

• Cenchreae

CYPRUS

Tripolis •

• Sparta

Paphos

Sidon •

• Damascus

Tyre •

CRETE

Caesarea •

Mediterranean
Sea

Jerusalem •

Alexandria •

ARABIA
(PETRAEA)

• Cyrene

EGYPT

Travelers: Paul, Barnabas, John Mark

Distance: 1,400 miles (2,253 km)

Dates: AD 47–49

1. **Antioch of Syria:** The Holy Spirit sends Paul and Barnabas to be missionaries. John Mark goes along as their helper. Acts 13:1–4

2. **Paphos:** Paul confronts a sorcerer and blinds him. Acts 13:5–12

3. **Perga:** John Mark leaves the group and returns to Jerusalem. Acts 13:13

4. **Antioch of Pisidia:** Paul preaches his longest recorded sermon, and many become believers. Jewish leaders drive Paul and Barnabas out of the city and the Lord calls Paul to focus his ministry on gentiles. Acts 13:14–52

5. **Iconium:** Plots against their lives force them to flee. Acts 14:1–7

6. **Lystra:** When Paul heals a lame man, the townspeople think he and Barnabas are Greek gods. Jews from Antioch and Iconium stir up the crowd, and Paul is stoned and left for dead outside the city. But he survives and goes back into the city. Acts 14:8–20

7. **Derbe:** Many disciples are added to the church. Acts 14:20–21

8. **Derbe to Antioch of Syria:** On the return trip, Paul and Barnabas appoint elders in the churches they had planted. Acts 14:21–25

9. **Antioch of Syria:** Paul and Barnabas report all that God had done. Acts 14:26–28

Paul's Second Missionary Journey

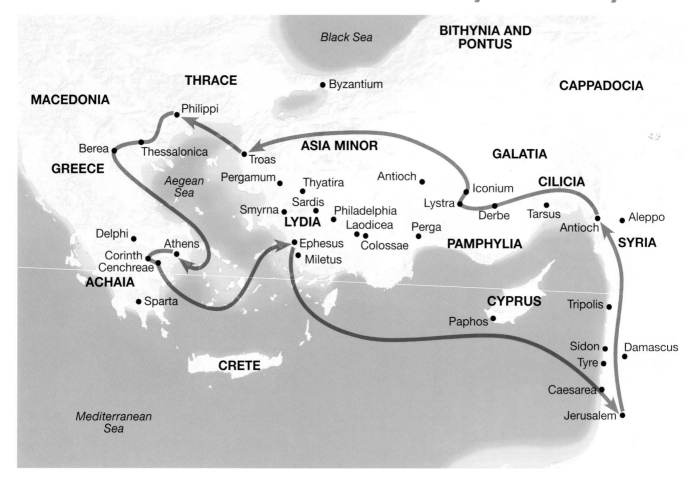

Travelers: Paul, Silas, Timothy, Luke, Priscilla and Aquila

Distance: 2,800 miles (4,506 km)

Dates: AD 49–51

1. **Antioch of Syria:** Paul and Barnabas disagree about who should go with them. Barnabas takes John Mark with him to Cyprus. Paul takes Silas. Acts 15:36–40

2. **Cilicia:** Paul and Silas deliver a letter from the Jerusalem church. Acts 15:41 (See Acts 15:22–29.)

3. **Lystra:** Timothy joins them. Acts 16:1–7

4. **Troas:** Paul has a vision of a man from Macedonia calling him to come help people there. So they head westward into Macedonia. Acts 16:8–10

5. **Philippi:** Lydia, a wealthy businesswoman, becomes a Christian. When a fortune-telling slave girl also becomes a Christian, her owners start a riot, and Paul and Silas are thrown in jail. After an earthquake, Paul and Silas stay in their cells. The jailer also becomes a believer. Acts 16:11–40

6. **Thessalonica:** A mob in Thessalonica tries to have Paul and Silas arrested. Acts 17:1–9

7. **Berea:** Silas and Timothy stay here while Paul goes on. Acts 17:10–15

8. **Athens:** Paul sees an altar to an unknown god and preaches to the philosophers at the Areopagus (Mars Hill). Acts 17:16–34

9. **Corinth:** Silas and Timothy rejoin Paul. He meets Priscilla and Aquila, who also join him. Acts 18:1–17

10. **Cenchreae:** Paul gets his hair cut because he had taken a vow. Acts 18:18

11. **Ephesus:** Paul establishes a local church, leaving Priscilla and Aquila to tend to it. Acts 18:19–21

12. **Antioch of Syria:** Paul returns to his home base of Antioch by way of Jerusalem. Acts 18:22

Paul's Third Missionary Journey

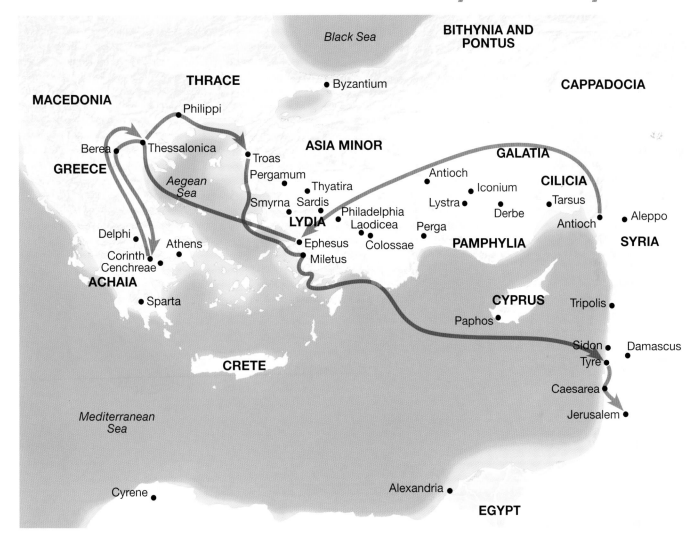

Travelers: Paul, Timothy, Luke, and others

Distance: 2,700 miles (4,345 km)

Dates: AD 52–57

1. **Galatia:** Paul visits the churches in this region. Acts 18:23

2. **Ephesus:** Paul stays here two years. So many people convert to Christianity that the silversmiths who manufacture idols start a riot. Acts 19:1–41

3. **Macedonia and Greece:** Paul gives encouraging words to believers in this region. He stays three months. Acts 20:1–3

4. **Troas:** While Paul is preaching, a young man falls asleep, falls from a third-story window, and dies. Paul revives him. Acts 20:4–12

5. **Miletus:** Elders from Ephesus meet the ship at Miletus and Paul tells them that he expects to be imprisoned in Jerusalem. Acts 20:13–38

6. **Tyre:** Believers warn Paul not to go to Jerusalem. Acts 21:1–6

7. **Caesarea:** A prophet predicts that Paul will be imprisoned and handed over to the gentiles. Acts 21:7–16

8. **Jerusalem:** Paul and his team report to the church leaders, who urge Paul to participate in a purification ritual at the temple to counteract rumors that Christianity is anti-Jewish. Acts 21:17–26

Paul's Journey to Rome

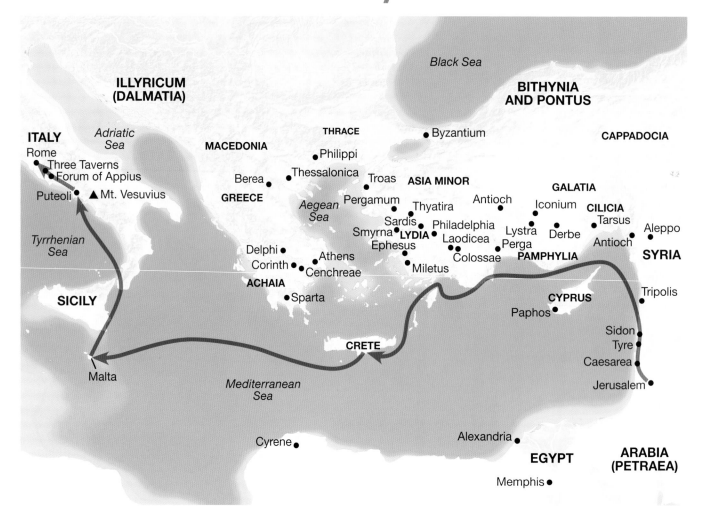

Travelers: Paul, Roman guards, Luke, and others

Distance: 2,250 miles (3,621 km)

Dates: AD 59–60

1. **Jerusalem:** After Paul is arrested, the Roman commander learns of a death threat against Paul, so he orders an armed escort to take Paul to Caesarea. Acts 23:12–35

2. **Caesarea:** Paul is tried before governor Felix, but Felix leaves him in prison for two years. Paul again stands trial, but this time before Festus, the new governor. Paul demands his right as a Roman citizen and appeals his case to Caesar. Herod Agrippa II visits Festus, and Paul appears before him as well. It's decided that Paul should go to Rome. Acts 24:1–26:32

3. **Sidon:** The centurion in charge of Paul lets him visit with friends. Then Paul boards a ship and sets sail for Rome. Acts 27:1–4

4. **Crete:** Paul recommends that the ship stay in safe harbor, but the centurion orders the ship to sail on. Acts 27:5–12

5. **Malta:** After a two-week storm, the ship is wrecked near the island of Malta. Everyone on the ship makes it to shore. Acts 27:13–28:10

6. **Puteoli:** Paul stays with believers for a week. Acts 28:11–14

7. **Forum of Appius and Three Taverns:** Paul is met by believers from Rome. Acts 28:15

8. **Rome:** Paul remains under house arrest for two years sharing the gospel with everyone he can. Acts 28:16–31

Acts

Time/Place
Acts tells the story (or the "acts") of the Holy Spirit working in the first Christians to spread the good news of Jesus from Jerusalem, Judea, Samaria, and to the world, covering about AD 30–62.

The Book
Written by Luke, Acts picks up where the gospel of Luke left off, with Jesus' ascension into heaven. The first twelve chapters focus on Peter and the apostles in Jerusalem, Judea, and Samaria. The remaining chapters detail Paul's journeys throughout the Mediterranean, and end with Paul in Rome.

Key Verse
"You will be my witnesses in Jerusalem, and in all of Judea and Samaria, and to the ends of the earth" (Acts 1:8).

James

Time/Place
James, the brother of Jesus, wrote this letter to Jewish believers scattered across the Roman Empire, about AD 49.

James was martyred in Jerusalem about thirteen years later in AD 62.

The Book
This short and very practical letter encourages believers to have an active, living faith that perseveres through all kinds of trials. James addresses issues like arrogance, favoritism, wealth, the impact of words, and serving others in need.

Key Verse
"As the body without the spirit is dead, so faith without deeds is dead" (James 2:26).

Galatians

Time/Place
Possibly the earliest of Paul's epistles, this letter was written to churches in Galatia from Paul's home base of Antioch of Syria, about AD 49, before the Jerusalem Council in Acts 15.

The Book
Paul defends his authority as an apostle and argues that the true gospel teaches that justification is by faith alone. People are saved by faith, not by good works or by obeying religious laws. This freedom, however, should be used to walk in the Spirit and not in the sinful desires of the flesh.

Key Verse
"A person is not justified by the works of the law, but by faith in Jesus Christ" (Gal. 2:16).

1 Thessalonians

Time/Place
Paul wrote his first letter to the church in Thessalonica during his second missionary journey, about AD 50–51.

The Book
Paul and Silas had earlier been forced to leave Thessalonica by an angry mob (see Acts 17:1–10). Paul spends the first part of this letter explaining his actions and absence. Then, he encourages believers to live holy lives, despite persecution, because Christ is coming again.

Key Verse
"For the Lord himself will come down from heaven . . . with the trumpet call of God, and the dead in Christ will rise first" (1 Thess. 4:16).

2 Thessalonians

Time/Place
Paul wrote his second letter to the church in Thessalonica during his second missionary journey, about AD 50–51, only six months after the first letter.

The Book
This second letter echoes many themes from the first letter. Paul clears up misunderstandings the Thessalonians had about the second coming of Christ and about those who pass away before Christ's return. Paul warns believers not to be idle, but to be prepared for Christ to come again.

Key Verse
"Stand firm and hold fast to the teachings we passed on to you" (2 Thess. 2:15).

1 Corinthians

Time/Place
Paul wrote this letter to the church in Corinth during his third missionary journey, about AD 55–56. Paul had founded the Corinthian church just a few years earlier on his second missionary trip (Acts 18:1–11).

The Book
Paul addresses various problems in the church, like division and immorality. He tells believers to love one another and to use their spiritual gifts to build each other up, for they are all one body in Christ.

Key Verse
"Love is patient, love is kind. It does not envy, it does not boast, it is not proud. . . . Love never fails" (1 Cor. 13:4, 8).

2 Corinthians

Time/Place
Paul wrote this letter to the church in Corinth during his third missionary journey, about AD 56, not long after 1 Corinthians.

The Book
This is Paul's most personal epistle. The problems addressed in 1 Corinthians were apparently not resolved. So, in this letter, Paul reinforces what he had taught earlier, and he offers a passionate defense of his ministry in the face of many attacks.

Key Verse
"[The Lord] said to me, 'My grace is sufficient for you, for my power is made perfect in weakness.' Therefore I will boast all the more gladly about my weaknesses, so that Christ's power may rest on me" (2 Cor. 12:9).

Romans

Time/Place
Paul wrote this letter to the church in Rome at the end of his third missionary journey, about AD 57. This was just before he went to Jerusalem, where he was taken captive and eventually brought to Rome in chains.

The Book
This is Paul's longest and most theological epistle. He discusses crucial topics of the Christian faith: law and the Spirit; sin and righteousness; condemnation and salvation. These truths should lead to transformed lives—"living sacrifices" to God (Rom. 12:1–2).

Key Verse
"For the wages of sin is death, but the gift of God is eternal life in Christ Jesus our Lord" (Rom. 6:23).

Ephesians

Time/Place
Paul wrote this letter to the church in Ephesus while under house arrest in Rome, about AD 60–62.

The Book
Paul had spent two years with the Ephesian Christians on his third missionary journey, so he knew their struggles up close. They faced tremendous pressure to participate in the sinfulness of their pagan surroundings. Paul urges believers to resist that pressure and to seize onto the riches of God's grace in Christ.

Key Verse
"For it is by grace you have been saved, through faith—and this is not from yourselves, it is the gift of God" (Eph. 2:8–9).

Philippians

Time/Place
Paul wrote this letter to the church in Philippi while under house arrest in Rome, about AD 60–62. Many people had become Christians in Philippi when Paul had visited the city on his second missionary journey.

The Book
Paul urges believers to "have the same mind-set as Christ" (Phil. 2:5) and to live humbly toward one another so that there is unity in the church.

Key Verse
". . . being confident of this, that he who began a good work in you will carry it on to completion until the day of Christ Jesus" (Phil. 1:6).

Colossians

Time/Place
Paul wrote this letter to the church in Colossae while under house arrest in Rome, about AD 60–62. Paul intended the letter also to be read to the nearby church in Laodicea (Col. 4:16).

The Book
Paul argues against a legalism that requires gentile Christians to follow Jewish religious laws. He dispels false teachings by emphasizing the supremacy of Christ over all human actions and philosophies.

Key Verse
"In Christ all the fullness of the Deity lives in bodily form, and in Christ you have been brought to fullness. He is the head over every power and authority" (Col. 2:9–10).

Philemon

Time/Place
Paul wrote this letter to Philemon, a wealthy leader in the church in Colossae, while under house arrest in Rome, about AD 60–62. This letter was probably sent along with the epistle of Colossians.

The Book
This is Paul's shortest epistle, only 25 verses. In it, he directly appeals to Philemon to accept a runaway slave, Onesimus, back as a brother in Christ. Verse 10 suggests that Onesimus had met Paul and became a Christian, and apparently wished for reconciliation with his old master.

Key Verse
"You might have him back forever—no longer as a slave, but . . . as a dear brother" (Philem. 15–16).

Jesus is crucified, resurrected, and ascends to heaven.
Acts 1:1–11

Matthias is chosen to be an apostle.
Acts 1:12–26

Pentecost: Holy Spirit fills disciples; 3,000 are saved.
Acts 2

Peter and John perform miracles and face persecution.
Acts 3–5

First Christian Martyr: Stephen is killed in Jerusalem.
Acts 6–7

AD 32

AD 30

Peter cites Psalms 69:25 and 109:8 as reasons for selecting another apostle.

Jesus had promised an advocate (the Spirit) to "be with you forever" and that the disciples would be "baptized with the Holy Spirit."
John 14:16; Acts 1:5

"I will pour out my Spirit on all people."
Joel 2:28–32

Jesus said, "If the world hates you, keep in mind that it hated me first. . . . They will treat you this way because of my name." John 15:18–21

Herod Agrippa has James (John's brother) put to death and imprisons Peter.
Acts 12:1–19

Herod Agrippa dies.
Acts 12:20–24

First Missionary Journey: Paul and Barnabas
Acts 13–14

Jerusalem Council: Gentiles are not required to obey Jewish religious laws.
Acts 15

Second Missionary Journey: Paul, Silas, and others.
Acts 16–18

AD 44

AD 47–49

AD 49

AD 49–51

AD 50

TIME LINE KEY

 Words of Jesus Fulfilled

 Old Testament Prophecy

 Book of the Bible Written

Dates are approximate.

James (Jesus' brother) writes his epistle.

At the council, James cites Amos 9:11–12 about how gentiles are included in God's plan.

Paul writes 1 and 2 Thessalonians.

Paul writes Galatians.

160

Persecution causes believers to disperse.
Acts 8:1–4

Philip preaches in Samaria and baptizes an Ethiopian man.
Acts 8:5–40

Conversion of Saul (Paul)
Acts 9:1–19

AD **37**

Saul's early travels.
Acts 9:20–31; Gal. 1:15–18

Peter takes the gospel to Cornelius; gentiles are filled with the Spirit.
Acts 10–11

AD **40**

The disciples become witnesses in Judea and Samaria just as Jesus said. Acts 1:8

The Ethiopian man was reading Isaiah 53:7–8, which told of the suffering Messiah, a prophecy Jesus fulfilled.

Isaiah prophesied that the Messiah would be "a light for the Gentiles." Isa. 42:6; Luke 2:32

Third Missionary Journey: Paul, Timothy, and others.
Acts 19–21

AD **52–57**

Paul is arrested, appears before Felix, and spends two years in prison.
Acts 21–24

Paul appears before Festus, Herod Agrippa II, and appeals his case to Caesar.
Acts 25–26

Journey to Rome: Paul is sent to Rome to stand trial.
Acts 27–28

AD **59–60**

Paul spends two years under house arrest in Rome and shares the gospel.
Acts 28:30–31

AD **60–62**

AD **60**

Paul writes 1 and 2 Corinthians, and Romans.

The Lord said Paul would proclaim Christ's name to kings. Acts 9:15

While in prison, the Lord had revealed to Paul that he would testify about Christ in Rome. Acts 23:11

Luke writes the gospel of Luke and the book of Acts.

Paul writes Ephesians, Philippians, Colossians, and Philemon.

CHAPTER 12

An Unfinished Story

From the End of Acts to the End of Time
AD 60–100

Paul's Final Years

The Apostle John

Latter Epistles and Revelation

Views of the End Times

In the final chapter of the book of Acts, Paul is under house arrest in Rome awaiting trial. The ending of Acts is less of a conclusion and more of a cliffhanger. This is fitting, since the gospel was only getting started. Jesus had promised to build his church by sending his Spirit to empower believers to take the gospel to the world (Matt. 16:18; Acts 1:8). Amazingly, in less than thirty-five years—with no television, radio, printing press, or internet—the gospel had transformed lives in Jerusalem, Judea, and Samaria, and across parts of Asia and Europe and all the way to Rome! But most of the world had still not heard the good news of Jesus. The rest of this story was yet to happen.

After the Book of Acts

1 and 2 Timothy; Titus

What happened in the decades following Acts can be pieced together from clues in the epistles written during this time, Christian tradition, and the historical record. While we don't know everything about Paul's final years, the most accepted theory is that after two years of house arrest, Paul was released

and allowed to travel again. From Paul's epistles written to Timothy and Titus, we know that he visited churches in Macedonia, Troas, Miletus, Crete, and Nicopolis (1 Tim. 1:3; 2 Tim. 4:13, 20; Titus 1:5; 3:12). The early church leader Clement said that Paul did fulfill his desire to go Spain, expressed in Romans 15:28, but whether the visit actually took place remains uncertain.

But after just a few years, Paul ended up in prison in Rome. By the time he returned to the city, Emperor Nero had already begun a brutal persecution of Christians. Paul's imprisonment this time was not house arrest. Rather, it's believed to have been in the cold, infamous Mamertine Prison, where the apostle Peter might also have been held. Some information about Paul's final days can be gleaned from his second letter to Timothy, written from prison. From this personal, heartfelt epistle, we know that Paul was visited by Onesiphorus, who "often refreshed

PETER'S STORY AFTER ACTS

The last mention of Peter in the book Acts is at the Jerusalem Council in AD 49 (Acts 15:7). But Peter had been known to travel widely spreading the gospel, and he likely continued to do so late in life (Gal. 2:9).

It appears he spent his final years ministering in Rome. Around AD 64, he wrote two back-to-back epistles (1 and 2 Peter) to encourage Christians facing suffering. It was a much-needed message not only for others, but also for Peter who would pay the ultimate price for his faith in Christ (John 21:18–19). Like Paul, Peter was imprisoned and martyred in Rome during Nero's persecution of Christians, around AD 66–68. According to tradition, Peter was crucified upside down, believing himself unworthy to be executed in the same manner as his Lord Jesus.

St. Paul in Prison by Rembrandt, 1627

me and was not ashamed of my chains" (2 Tim. 1:16–17). But we also know that Paul had been abandoned by many Christians when he stood trial (2 Tim. 4:10, 16). Luke alone was still with Paul, although Paul expressed the hope that he would see John Mark again when Timothy came to visit (2 Tim. 4:11).

Historical evidence suggests that Paul was executed in Rome, around AD 66–68. According to tradition, he was beheaded on the Ostian Way, a road just outside the city.

The Lord had chosen Paul on the road to Damascus some thirty years prior, and Paul had chosen to follow the Lord wherever he led, even when that path led to suffering. Yet Paul learned to be content and even joyful in his circumstances. He knew—and could reassure the Christians he wrote to—that "my God will meet all your needs according to the riches of his glory in Christ Jesus" (Phil. 4:19). In Paul's last epistle, he wrote, "The time for my departure is near. I have fought the good fight, I have finished the race, I have kept the faith. Now there is in store for me the crown of righteousness, which the Lord, the righteous Judge, will award to me on that day—and not only to me, but also to all who have longed for his appearing" (2 Tim. 4:6–8).

APOCALYPTIC WRITINGS

Apocalyptic writings in the Bible reveal God's hidden plans through visions, symbols, and images. The word *apocalypse* comes from a Greek word meaning "unveiling" or "uncovering." It's this word in Revelation 1:1 that is translated in most English Bibles as "revelation." In biblical times, apocalyptic writings often came out of periods of intense suffering and persecution. These writings included messages of judgment, but also of hope for a coming restoration. The book of Ezekiel, many of Daniel's prophecies, and the book of Revelation are apocalyptic.

The Apostle John

1, 2 and 3 John; Revelation 1–20

John was a young man (probably still a teenager) when he first encountered Jesus, but by the time he wrote his epistles near the end of the first century, he was an elderly man who had seen so much over the years.

As one of the original twelve disciples, John had been with Jesus since the beginning of his ministry. John walked with, ate with, and listened to Jesus. He learned from the Master. Yet he had also run in fear for his own life when Jesus was arrested, and he witnessed his Lord be crucified like a criminal. John was one of the first disciples to see the empty tomb. Later, he witnessed his Lord alive and risen from the grave! It was just as Jesus had told him: "Your grief will turn to joy" (John 16:20).

After Christ's ascension, John saw God do miraculous things through the church (Acts 3:1–10). But he also knew the persecution that the church faced, and felt the sorrow of losing his own brother to martyrdom (Acts 12:2). Nevertheless, in

John's epistles, we see a man assured of eternal life in Christ: "I write these things to you who believe in the name of the Son of God so that you may know that you have eternal life" (1 John 5:13). John trusted in God's power to overcome sin and evil: "The one who is in you is greater than the one who is in the world" (1 John 4:4).

John's final writing was the book of Revelation. He received this revelation while exiled for his faith on the island of Patmos. (The Romans would often banish political prisoners

to Patmos and surrounding islands.) During this exile, John received visions from God— just as the ancient prophets Daniel and Ezekiel had received visions while Israel was in exile. Through signs, symbols, and other imagery, God revealed to John what was yet to come and, especially, of the victorious reign of Jesus Christ.

In chapter seven of Revelation, John describes a scene in which he was allowed to see into heaven itself:

> A great multitude that no one could count, from every nation, tribe, people and language, standing before the throne and before the Lamb. They were wearing white robes and were holding palm branches in their hands. And they cried out in a loud voice: "Salvation belongs to our God, who sits on the throne, and to the Lamb." (Rev. 7:9–10)

As the risen Christ had told his disciples, repentance and forgiveness of sins would be preached to all nations (Luke 24:47; Acts 1:8). This scene from Revelation shows that God's plan cannot and will not be thwarted. The book of Revelation—the last book of the Bible—is ultimately a message of hope.

Historical evidence suggests that John was eventually released from exile. He lived the remainder of his days with Christians in Ephesus where he died of natural causes, the last of the twelve apostles to exit this world for the next.

St. John the Evangelist by Juan Ribalta, c. 1618

1 Timothy

Time/Place
Paul wrote this letter to Timothy, a young pastor in Ephesus, about AD 62–66.

The Book
Paul gives instructions to Timothy about proper worship and church leadership, and how to deal with false teachings in the church.

In this letter, we see Paul, who was advanced in years, passing the torch to a younger Christian leader, encouraging Timothy to "fight the good fight of the faith" (1 Tim. 6:12).

Key Verse
"Don't let anyone look down on you because you are young, but set an example for the believers in speech, in conduct, in love, in faith and in purity" (1 Tim. 4:12).

Titus

Time/Place
Paul wrote this letter to Titus, about AD 64–66. This was after Paul had been released from house arrest, but before his second confinement in Rome.

Titus was a gentile convert who was in charge of churches on the Island of Crete. He had travelled with Paul years earlier (Gal. 2:1–5).

The Book
Paul provides instructions about responsible church leadership, correct doctrine, and living in God's grace and mercy.

Key Verse
"When the kindness and love of God our Savior appeared, he saved us, not because of righteous things we had done, but because of his mercy" (Titus 3:4–5).

2 Timothy

Time/Place
Paul wrote this letter to Timothy, about AD 66–67. This was Paul's last epistle. He wrote it while imprisoned in Rome.

The Book
Paul encourages Timothy to remain faithful in ministry despite hardships.

Paul concludes the letter by expressing how he feels deserted by some believers during his imprisonment. He says Luke is still with him and he looks forward to Timothy visiting him soon (2 Tim. 4:9–18).

Key Verse
"The time for my departure is near. I have fought the good fight, I have finished the race, I have kept the faith" (2 Tim. 4:6–7).

TIMOTHY

Timothy had been invited to travel with Paul when Paul passed through Lystra on his second missionary journey.

Timothy's father was a Greek and his mother was a Jewish Christian (Acts 16:1). Both his mother Eunice and his grandmother Lois modeled a life of sincere faith and raised Timothy to live similarly (2 Tim. 1:5; 3:15).

He had been with Paul during Paul's house arrest in Rome (Phil. 1:1; Col. 1:1). Paul commended him saying, "I have no one else like him. . . . As a son with his father he has served with me in the work of the gospel" (Phil. 2:20–22).

1 Peter

Time/Place
Peter wrote this letter to Christians in Asia Minor who faced injustice, about AD 64. This was late in Peter's life, not long before he was executed in Emperor Nero's persecution of Christians.

The Book
Peter calls Christians to live holy lives and to be encouraged, knowing that Jesus also suffered unjustly in order to bring healing to all. Holy living in the midst of hardship is a testimony to a lost world.

Key Verse
"To this you were called, because Christ suffered for you, leaving you an example, that you should follow in his steps" (1 Peter 2:21).

2 Peter

Time/Place
Peter wrote this letter to Christians, possibly in Asia Minor, about AD 64, soon after 1 Peter was written.

The Book
Peter warns Christians about false teachers and encourages them to grow in their faith. He also assures readers that the prophetic word and apostolic testimony are not human creations, but are reliable testimonies. He reminds believers of Christ's promised return.

Key Verse
"The Lord is not slow in keeping his promise, as some understand slowness. Instead he is patient with you, not wanting anyone to perish, but everyone to come to repentance" (2 Peter 3:9).

Hebrews

Time/Place
This letter was written by an unknown author to a Jewish Christian audience facing persecution, about AD 60–69.

The Book
The message of Hebrews is that Jesus is superior to all things—to angels, the Old Testament prophets, the priesthood, and the sacrificial system. His death on the cross fulfilled the old covenant. He is the great High Priest, the final sacrifice, and the superior tabernacle. Believers enter into his promised land of rest through faith.

Key Verse
"Since we have a great high priest who has ascended into heaven, Jesus the Son of God, let us hold firmly to the faith we profess" (Heb. 4:14).

Jude

Time/Place
Jude wrote this letter to Christians everywhere in the latter part of the first century, sometime in the AD 60s–80s. (The exact date of Jude is difficult to determine.)

Jude may have been the brother of Jesus who is called Judas in Matthew 13:55.

The Book
This short letter encourages believers to contend for the faith by resisting false teachings and helping other Christians to do the same.

Key Verse
"To him who is able to keep you from stumbling and to present you before his glorious presence without fault and with great joy" (Jude 24).

1 John

Time/Place

The apostle John wrote this letter to several churches in Asia Minor, about AD 85–95.

The Book

This is the longest of John's three epistles. In this letter, he focuses on God's love through Jesus and our love for one another.

Also, some false teachers in the church were claiming that Jesus only appeared to be human. John refutes such claims and affirms Jesus' full humanity.

Key Verse

"This is how we know what love is: Jesus Christ laid down his life for us. And we ought to lay down our lives for our brothers and sisters" (1 John 3:16).

2 John

Time/Place

John wrote this letter to "the lady chosen by God"—possibly an expression meaning "the church"—about AD 85–95. Like John's other epistles, this short letter was probably sent to churches in Asia Minor.

The Book

John reminds Christians that love, which means obeying God's instructions, also includes being discerning, so that Christians will not be deceived by false teachings.

Key Verse

"I am not writing you a new command but one we have had from the beginning. I ask that we love one another. And this is love: that we walk in obedience to his commands" (2 John 5–6).

3 John

Time/Place

John wrote this letter to Gaius, a Christian in Asia Minor, about AD 85–95.

In both 2 John and 3 John, the author calls himself "the elder."

The Book

This is the shortest book of the New Testament, only thirteen verses.

In this letter, John commends Gaius for his love, faithfulness, and hospitality. But John also denounces Diotrephes for acting arrogantly, gossiping, and refusing to welcome other believers.

Key Verse

"I have no greater joy than to hear that my children are walking in the truth" (3 John 4).

Revelation

Time/Place

John received this revelation while he was exiled on the island of Patmos for his faith, about AD 95. The book is addressed to seven churches in Asia Minor.

The Book

Revelation is presented in a series of "sevens," a number of completion. John is given seven messages for seven churches. He has visions of seven seals, seven bowls, seven trumpets, and so forth. This book reminds believers that even when evil seems strong, God is in control of history. One day, the Lord will renew his creation and dwell with his people for eternity.

Key Verse

"There will be no more death or mourning or crying or pain, for the old order of things has passed away" (Rev. 21:4).

Seven Churches of Revelation

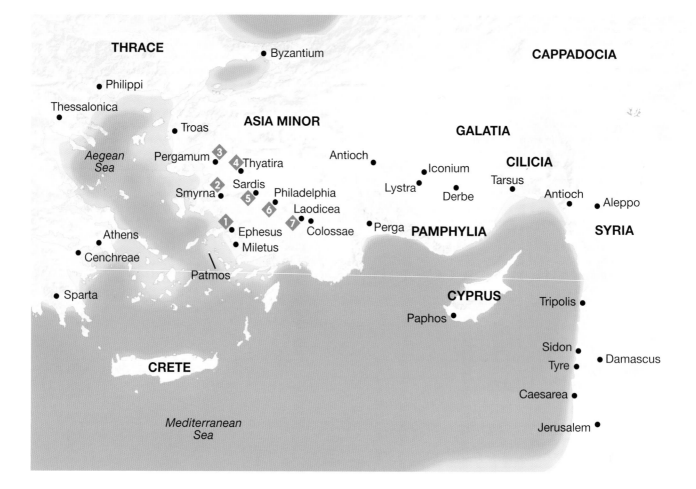

	Church	Strengths	Weaknesses	Instruction	Promise
1	Ephesus Rev. 2:1–7	Perseverance; reject false teachers	Forsaken their first love	Do the things they did at first	Eat from the tree of life
2	Smyrna Rev. 2:8–11	Endure suffering and poverty, yet are rich	None	Be faithful to the point of death	Life as a victor's crown
3	Pergamum Rev. 2:12–17	True to Christ's name	Tolerate false teachers	Repent	Hidden manna; a new name
4	Thyatira Rev. 2:18–29	Deeds, love, faith, and service	Tolerate false prophets	Hold on to what they have	Authority; the morning star
5	Sardis Rev. 3:1–6	Some have remained faithful	Deadness	Strengthen what remains; wake up	Walk with Jesus; name in the book of life
6	Philadelphia Rev. 3:7–13	Kept Christ's word; not denied his name	None	Hold on to what they have	Kept from hour of trial; pillar in God's temple
7	Laodicea Rev. 3:14–22	None	Neither hot nor cold; trust in wealth	Open the door to Christ; buy riches from Christ	Sit with Christ on God's throne

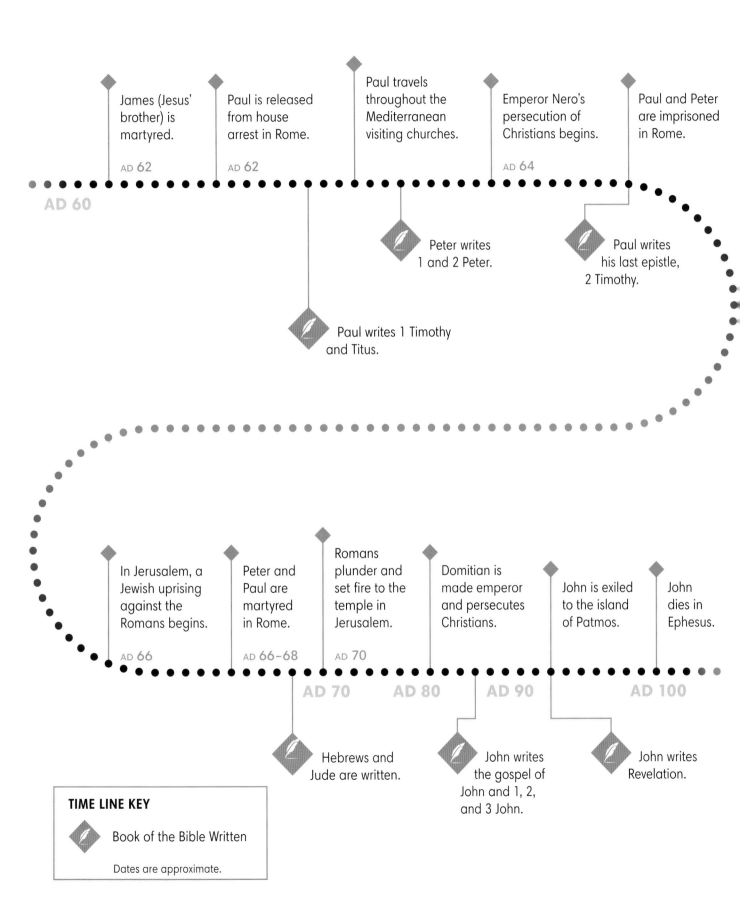

James (Jesus' brother) is martyred.

AD 62

Paul is released from house arrest in Rome.

AD 62

Paul travels throughout the Mediterranean visiting churches.

Emperor Nero's persecution of Christians begins.

AD 64

Paul and Peter are imprisoned in Rome.

Peter writes 1 and 2 Peter.

Paul writes his last epistle, 2 Timothy.

Paul writes 1 Timothy and Titus.

AD 60

In Jerusalem, a Jewish uprising against the Romans begins.

AD 66

Peter and Paul are martyred in Rome.

AD 66–68

Romans plunder and set fire to the temple in Jerusalem.

AD 70

Domitian is made emperor and persecutes Christians.

John is exiled to the island of Patmos.

John dies in Ephesus.

AD 70   AD 80   AD 90   AD 100

Hebrews and Jude are written.

John writes the gospel of John and 1, 2, and 3 John.

John writes Revelation.

TIME LINE KEY

Book of the Bible Written

Dates are approximate.

171

Views of the End Times

After Christ's ascension into heaven, the angels present assured the disciples, "[He] will come back in the same way you have seen him go into heaven" (Acts 1:11). But when will his second coming be? Jesus said "that day or hour no one knows" (Mark 13:32), but he also gave signs to watch for (Matt. 23–24). He urged his followers to "Be on guard!" and "Be alert!" (Mark 13:33, 37). Over the centuries, Christians have held different beliefs about what events might happen in the end times and in what order. Here are four main Christian views.

Historical Premillennialism

This is the belief that Christians will remain on the earth during the great tribulation (Rev. 7:14), which will purify the churches by rooting out false believers. The second coming of Christ will precede the millennium (Rev. 20:4–6), which is a literal, future event. God's promises of land and blessings to Abraham and his offspring were conditional promises based on their obedience. The church has replaced the nation of Israel as God's covenant people. God has maintained a covenant of grace throughout the Old and New Testaments with all who trusted in him. These believers—embodied today in the church—are the true Israel (Rom. 9:6–8; Gal. 6:16).

Dispensational Premillennialism

This is the belief that Jesus will come back to earth after a seven-year tribulation and will rule during a thousand-year millennium of peace on earth. God will still give to the nation of Israel the land described (Gen. 15:18). All references to Israel in Revelation refer to the nation of Israel. Most who hold this view are pre-tribulationists; they understand Revelation 4:1–2 to refer to the rapture. The rapture is the event when Christ removes Christians from the earth before the great tribulation begins (1 Thess. 4:15–17). The rapture and the second coming of Jesus are two separate events. Others who hold this view are mid-tribulationists; they believe the rapture will occur during the tribulation.

Amillennialism

This is the belief that the millennium is the spiritual reign of Jesus in the hearts of his followers. The "first resurrection" (Rev. 20:5) is not a physical restoration from the dead, but a spiritual resurrection (regeneration). Christ's triumph over Satan through his death and resurrection restrained the power of Satan on earth (Rev. 20:1–3). Persecution of Christians (tribulation) will occur until Jesus comes again, as will the expansion of God's kingdom (the millennium). When Christ returns, he will immediately defeat the powers of evil, resurrect the saved and the unsaved, judge them, and deliver them to their eternal destinies.

Postmillennialism

This is the belief that the second coming of Christ will occur after the millennium, which represents a long time period when, through the preaching of the gospel, most of the world will submit to Jesus (Rev. 19:19–20:3). Christ will rule the earth through his Spirit and church. Some view the tribulation as a brief period immediately before the millennium, and others view it as having already occurred in the first century. The resurrection in Revelation 20:4 represents the spiritual regeneration of people who trust in Jesus. The second coming, the final conflict between good and evil, the defeat of Satan, the physical resurrection of all people, and the final judgment will occur together, after the millennium (Rev. 20:7–15).

HISTORICAL PREMILLENNIALISM

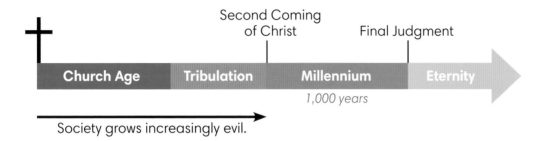

DISPENSATIONAL PREMILLENNIALISM

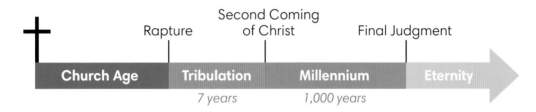

AMILLENNIALISM

POSTMILLENNIALISM

Imagery in the Book of Revelation

Imagery	Revelation	Old Testament
Son of Man Coming in the Clouds	Rev. 1:7, 13	Dan. 7:13
One Who Is Pierced	Rev. 1:7	Zech. 12:10
Alpha and Omega/First and Last	Rev. 1:8; 21:6; 22:13	Isa. 44:6; 48:12
Throne Room of God	Rev. 4:1–11	Isa. 6:1–3; Ezek. 1:4–28
Lion of the Tribe of Judah	Rev. 5:5	Gen. 49:9–10
Lamb Who Was Slain	Rev. 5:6–13	Ex. 12:1–13; Isa. 53:7
Horses and Riders	Rev. 6:2–8	Zech. 1:8; 6:1–6
No Hunger, Thirst, or Tears	Rev. 7:16–17; 21:4	Isa. 25:8; 49:10
Shepherd	Rev. 7:17	Ezek. 34:11–31
Swarm of Locusts	Rev. 9:3–11	Ex. 10:12–15; Joel 1:4; 2:25
Eating a Scroll	Rev. 10:9–11	Ezek. 2:9–3:3
Measuring the Temple	Rev. 11:1	Ezek. 40:3
Michael the Archangel	Rev. 12:7	Dan. 10:13
Serpent	Rev. 12:7–9	Gen. 3:1; Isa. 27:1
Beasts from the Sea	Rev. 13:1–2	Dan. 7:2–7
Foreheads Marked	Rev. 13:16–17; 14:1	Ezek. 9:4
Mount Zion	Rev. 14:1	Isa. 2:3; Zech. 8:3
Temple Filled with Smoke/Cloud	Rev. 15:8	Ex. 40:34; Isa. 6:4
Armageddon/Megiddo	Rev. 16:16	Judg. 5:19; Zech. 12:11
Adulterous Woman	Rev. 17:1–2	Ezek. 16:30–32
Wedding	Rev. 19:7; 21:2	Isa. 54:5–7; 61:10
Thrones of Judgment	Rev. 20:4, 11	Dan. 7:9–10
Gog and Magog	Rev. 20:7–10	Ezek. 38:2
Book of Life	Rev. 20:12	Ps. 69:28; Dan. 7:10; 12:1
New Heaven and New Earth	Rev. 21:1	Isa. 65:17; 66:22
God's Dwelling Place	Rev. 21:3–4	Ex. 29:45; Ezek. 37:27
Holy City Made of Jewels	Rev. 21:18–21	Isa. 54:11–12
Open Gates	Rev. 21:21, 25	Isa. 60:11
Living Water	Rev. 22:1–2	Ezek. 47:1–2; Zech. 14:8
Tree of Life	Rev. 22:2, 14, 19	Gen. 2:9

New Heaven and New Earth

Revelation 21–22

Though Christians have different views about how the end times will unfold, there are some important points of agreement: Christ is coming back again and will judge humanity; the powers of evil are doomed before Christ; and God promises a wonderful future for all who trust in Christ.

The final two chapters of Revelation give us a glimpse into this future, a time when all things in this world marred by sin and evil will be restored to the life God intended for them since the beginning.

> Then I saw "a new heaven and a new earth," for the first heaven and the first earth had passed away. . . . And I heard a loud voice from the throne saying, "Look! God's dwelling place is now among the people, and he will dwell with them. They will be his people, and God himself will be with them and be their God. 'He will wipe every tear from their eyes. There will be no more death' or mourning or crying or pain, for the old order of things has passed away."
> (Rev. 21:1–4)

Many have understood this vision in Revelation to represent a restored garden of Eden. In the first chapter of the Bible, God creates "the heavens and the earth" (Gen. 1:1). In Revelation, he reveals a new heaven and new earth (Rev. 21:1). Adam and Eve ate from the tree that brought sin into the world instead of the tree of life (Gen. 2:9). In Revelation, the tree of life stands in the middle of the new holy city, bringing healing to the nations (Rev. 22:2).

It's the happy ending to the great story of God. This story is also our story. One day, sin will be abolished and death will be no more. In place of our tears and pain today, there will be infinite joy and life to the full. Lost souls from every "nation, tribe, people and language" will be redeemed (Rev. 7:9). Hard-hearted rebels will become whole-hearted worshipers. Those who were dead will live forever, face-to-face with Almighty God himself. Until that day comes, we draw encouragement from the stories of faithful men and women of God who have gone before us. We join in praise with our great King who says, "I am making everything new!" (Rev. 21:5).

Index